THE NEGLECTED

AND ABUSED

A PHYSICIAN'S YEAR IN HAITI

Joseph F. Bentivegna, M.D.

MICHELLE PUBLISHING COMPANY

ROCKY HILL, CT 06067

Bentivegna, Joseph Francis, 1956-

The Neglected and Abused
Includes Index and References
Library of Congress Catalog Card No. 90-6181
RA-456.H3 B44

Second Printing, 1991

 Second printing. Printed in the United States of America. Published by Michelle Publishing Company, Rocky Hill, CT.

ISBN 0-962-60010-5

DEDICATION

To the decent, hard-working people of Haiti.

AUTHOR'S NOTE

I would never have believed that I would sell enough books to require a second printing but here it is. I would like to take this opportunity to correct an egregious error in the first printing. I succumbed to the rumor that The Albert Schweitzer Hospital in central Haiti had closed. Nothing could be further from the truth. It continues to serve Haiti's poor and is a beacon to those of us who are optimistic about Haiti's future.

While it is impossible to list everyone who helped with the production of this book, I owe my eternal gratitude to Dr. Bryant Freeman, Professor of French and Director of Haitian Studies at The University of Kansas. Dr. Freeman meticulously corrected the numerous errors in the Creole statements in my first printing. His other comments were invaluable in enhancing the accuracy and quality of the second printing.

Joseph F. Bentivegna M.D.
Rocky Hill, Connecticut
November 10, 1991

Table of Contents

PREFACE

Upon completing my internship, I did something I had always wanted to do. I worked in a Third-World country as a physician, helping the poor with the skills I had studied long and diligently to acquire. I chose Haiti, which is located in the Caribbean, a few hundred miles southeast of Florida. It is the poorest country in the Western Hemisphere. With many people dying unnecessarily from tuberculosis, malaria and diarrhea, I felt that Haiti needed more doctors to work with these eminently treatable diseases. I cured many. I saved more lives than physicians who practice for a lifetime in the United States, but I came to realize I was fighting a losing battle. These diseases existed because of overpopulation, malnutrition, poor sanitation and ignorance, and I was doing nothing to address these problems. Rather than leave in despair, I continued to work and I wrote this book. I hope it will encourage others to help this poor but wonderful country.

Introduction

To help developing countries is no mere largesse. What better investment can the North make in its own future than by turning today's deprived South into tomorrow's customers?

Indira Gandhi

Why was I born in America?

I could have been a blind beggar in India, a Cambodian child helplessly watching his parents be slaughtered; or a Haitian mother with six children, no husband and pregnant. But, no. When the biological dice rolled, I got double sixes. I was born in an American middle class family where everything was handed to me. My major concern while growing up was whether or not the Yankees were winning. In college, I merely had to get good grades so that I could attend medical school. I never had to scrape for a meal or worry whether I had a place to sleep. No government police ever came to beat my parents, and when a president was accused of breaking the law, he was deposed without a shot being fired.

For most of this planet's five-billion inhabitants, this is not the case. One-third goes to sleep hungry. They are ravaged by diseases which waste their bodies, causing slow agonizing and degrading deaths. They are frozen by ignorance, illiteracy and insolvency in political and economic structures that offer them no chance to better their lives. When they are brutalized, or have their homes confiscated, they have no recourse.

These people live in the Third World, a group of non-industrialized nations located in Africa, Asia and South America. With few exceptions, the resources and pleasures of this planet pass them by. While more Americans are buying graphite tennis rackets, Gucci clothes and fine Bordeaux, the Third World is sliding from an attitude of pessimism to abject despair. While our population growth is slowing, they continue to produce masses of people they can neither feed nor house.

In the Third World, many die from treatable diseases such as tuberculosis, malaria, and diarrhea. Even the healthy are not safe from the ravages of polio and tetanus because vaccinations are not available. While $100,000 is spent to prolong the life of an American who is obviously dying, those in the Third World perish or are permanently crippled because a dollar's worth of medicine is unavailable.

Before going to Haiti, I never understood why the Third World was disintegrating. For example:

1. Why can't we not eradicate disease by sending more doctors?
2. With contraception available, why are birth rates so high?
3. Why do we pay farmers not to grow food while starvation exists?

With these questions in mind, I began to search for a Third-World country that needed my help. To my surprise, there were many opportunities. I could have worked in India, Pakistan or El Salvador, but none of these countries is as poor as Haiti.

My interest in Haiti was prompted by a Catholic priest, Father Normand Demers, a liberation theologian who espouses a controversial movement that stresses justice in the present life. Previously, the Church told the poor to tolerate their lot so their rewards in heaven would be greater. He combined the Gospel's message with our responsibility to alleviate poverty in the Third World. Fluent in Spanish and French and having visited over 70 countries, he had an immense knowledge of the world situation and a delightful variety of anecdotes.

A man of 5'10", he had a square jaw, carefully groomed, graying red hair, a pointed nose and friendly but cautious eyes. Solidly built, he had a clear complexion making him appear ten years younger than his actual age of 50. He impressed me as someone who could easily have been a successful lawyer or politician, and I suspect his principled opinions prevented him from advancing in the Church hierarchy. Over dinner, we discussed Haiti. He could arrange for me to work with two organizations in Haiti's capital, Port-au-Prince. One would be the Missionaries of Charity, the order of Mother Teresa; the other was a non-sectarian Dutch organization that needed a doctor to run its clinic. Physicians frequently volunteer in Haiti, but few spend other than brief sojourns. Consequently, they never become familiar with its diseases, its culture or its language, Creole. It was all arranged. His parish would sponsor me while I was a doctor in Haiti.

I did have second thoughts, though. Haiti is truly a a ravaged country. Once the most affluent colony of the French empire, it now has mass starvation, rampant overpopulation and an infant mortality rate of 15%. A large percentage of children die before age five. Various attempts by developed nations to assist have been met with continual frustration.

Institutionalized corruption siphons off foreign aid, so the needy are never helped. High export taxes discourage peasants from growing popular crops while politically influential families make huge profits because they are exempt from paying taxes. Five percent of the country, mostly the mulatto elite, make 50% of the income, while the yearly per capita income is $300. Illiterate and superstitious, most Haitians eke out a day-to-day existence hustling everything from avocadoes to their own bodies.

I would oversee two hospitals, one for adults and the other for children. Some patients just needed a place to stay because they had been crawling on the streets or had been rejected by other hospitals. Most were genuinely sick, from diarrhea, tuberculosis, malaria, and other diseases. All had malnutrition. Medicine and simple equipment were available, having been sent by charities or donated by drug companies unable to market them. My job would be to determine which patients would benefit from medical care, and then to see that they received proper treatment.

Typically, my day began at the Children's Home where there were 50 children from infancy to age 10. Some were healthy, and simply needed to eat, but others were sick and dying. After morning rounds, I drove to an outpatient clinic, battling the aggressive Haitian drivers with my 70 cc moped. I saw anywhere from 20 to 200 patients at the clinic. Here, I saved the most lives, either by explaining to a mother how to give electrolyte water to her dehydrated child or by draining abscesses before they spread their poison through the body. Then, I travelled to the hospital for adults or "Sans Fil," as it was called after a nearby street. There were over 150 patients, most with tuberculosis. I helped the ones I could. Exhausted when the day ended, I returned to my apartment and wrote what I had seen.

Overall, it was a great challenge. There were more patients than I could possibly have seen, and the more work I did, the more work I created. I established a vaccination program which was successfully administered by two young men. I became an old-time family doctor, relying on instinct, judgment, physical exam and the primitive laboratory tests that I performed. In one sense, it was the most satisfying experience of my life. But as time passed, I realized that people like me will not solve Haiti's problems. They can only be solved by the Haitians themselves.

Chapter 1

Haiti

Those who make peaceful revolution impossible make violent revolution inevitable.

John F. Kennedy

As the plane descended, I could not help but feel insane for coming here. Even from the air, Haiti reeks with despair. Throughout the rural areas, I could see makeshift huts that housed a dozen people. There were fallow fields and denuded mountains, ravaged by hungry peasants trying to cultivate unarable land. Over Port-au-Prince, the huge slums came into view. It was not until I landed that the blunt reality hit me. Nothing could have prepared me for the abject poverty and the stark contrasts I saw. The slides, the pictures, the talks, the magazine articles only intimated what it was really like. Now I saw it, in glorious three dimensions, complete with sound and smell.

I was thrust into the worst living conditions in the Western Hemisphere – the slums of Port-au-Prince. I visited the largest, Cité Simone, named after the mother of the former President-for-Life. Thousands upon thousands of unemployed rural peasants have crammed into this area. Occasional fires roar through, leaving many homeless. Around the periphery of the city, new slums are burgeoning. Some have been named after American cities such as Brooklyn and Boston. In the past 10 years, the population of Port-au-Prince has doubled to over 1,000,000. These slums spawn a multitude of disease-infested human beings – my patients.

Housing consists of shacks smaller than a college dormitory room made of wooden sticks with a hodgepodge of foliage, mud, animal dung and cardboard. Sheets of corrugated tin serve as roofs even though most have rust-eroded holes. A well-placed kick could easily flatten one. The better shacks also have metal sheets as siding and luxury complexes have cement bricks. The floors are coarse dirt, and because of overcrowding the occupants sleep in shifts. Naturally, there is no privacy and sex education in Haiti is by observation.

The main theme in this collage of despair is the conservation of space. Clothes lines are suspended between the shacks that appear incapable of supporting anything, lest the shacks be pulled down. Pans, kettles and shovels are stored on the roof-tops. Garbage is heaped up at the entrances, spewing into the narrow streets along with human excrement, orange and banana peels, scraps of sharp metal, cans, and broken glass imbedded in the mud. Puddles of stagnant water coalesce forming a stream—the sewage system. The slowly oozing water is covered by a thick brown reflective film occasionally pierced with proliferating green algae. It is quite popular with the flies. Emanating from it comes a hideous stench—a combination of excrement and decaying fruit fermenting in the 100-degree sun.

The most striking feature, though, is the masses of people, over 100,000 squashed in a square mile with one-story housing. Haiti is the most densely populated country in the Western Hemisphere, averaging 700 people per square mile as opposed to 50 in Nicaragua or 60 in the United States.

The Haitians are busy surviving. Everyone is hustling, jammed into the narrow streets performing the necessary chores of pre-industrial society. The women, dressed in colorful ankle length skirts and matching T-shirts, are carrying buckets of water, baskets of fruit or piles of clothing on their heads. Frequently, they are followed by a miniature, their daughter, doing the same. This method of transporting goods requires tremendous balance and coordination and is learned at an early age. These women are able to stop, turn their heads and even walk up stairs with 60-pound loads on their heads. It gives them stately posture and a buoyant lilt that accentuates their well-proportioned frames. It also gives them intense neck and back pain, a problem I would frequently treat.

Many women congregate around a large block with protruding pipes, the water source. Naked children abound with their shiny pot bellies, stick legs and red hair, a sign of malnutrition. Upon seeing me, they run up yelling "blan, blan," some with outstretched hands asking for money but most just curious to get a closer look at me. To the uninitiated, being called a "blan" or "white" seems insulting but in actuality the term is reserved for foreigners, including American blacks. When I mastered Creole, I became a "nèg," one of the guys.

Unlike the women, not all the men are working. Sex roles are well-defined and some would rather sit idly than carry water or cook. Most are hustling though. Shirtless in the brutal sun, wearing dull pants and laceless torn shoes, they pull carts with loaded cement bags or charcoal – Haiti's main source of energy. This toil results in elegantly sculptured torsos that no Nautilus machine could produce.

Amidst this activity are meatless animals – chickens, goats and dogs. Pigs, once Haiti's main scavenger, are conspicuously absent. They have been eradicated because some harbored African Swine Flu. The program ostensibly was to help Haiti, but in actuality was conceived to prevent the virus from spreading to the United States and endangering the multi-billion dollar pork industry.

As if this were not enough sensory overload, a white Mazda suddenly invades the street. An upper-class Haitian is driving, and he obnoxiously blasts his horn while accelerating. The women grab their produce and children, rapidly dispersing as the juggernaut speeds towards them. No one casts defiant glares but merely accepts this behavior as the right of the "gwo nèg," the "big shot."

Malere pa janm gin rezon devan gwo nèg.
The poor man has no rights before the big shot.

Walking towards central Port-au-Prince, I came to a market, the hub of the peasant economy where rural peasants sell their produce. The vendors are mostly women. They begin their trek early, arriving at daybreak, selling and bartering until dusk. Since marketing is also an important social event, a woman will not sell all her produce early in the day, even if offered twice its value.

Each vendor squats in carefully mapped-out territory, her colorful skirt draped between her legs protecting her modesty. Huge broad-brimmed hats shield them from the sun. Much of the attire is outmoded American clothing – bell bottoms, wide belts and paisley shirts. The Haitians call them "kennedies" after the American President who increased humanitarian aid to their country while surreptitiously attempting to overthrow its government.

All one needs to survive is here – mangoes, avocadoes, sugar cane, cornmeal, rice, meat, soap, clothing, and linen. Many potential customers are milling about but it looks as if everyone is selling but nobody is buying. The vendors have a low-key soft-sell approach for their fickle and impecunious customers. My presence changes this. With huge smiles, the vendors hold up their wares. To them, I am a "blan bet" or "stupid white" who pays four times the going price of an avocado, which is still one-third the price in the United States. After learning Creole, I became a "blan chich" or "cheap white," who insisted on paying the same price as the Haitians.

While scanning this scene, my eyes meet those of a woman who has five large baskets stacked on her head. Thinking of me as a customer rather than a curious onlooker, she stops by thrusting her hips forward and stopping them while letting her upper body gradually recoil forward in a serpentine fashion absorbing the movement of the baskets. When she raises her eyebrows towards her wares, I nod my head with the universal no. Grimacing, she repeats the serpentine movement and continues.

I was then taken to Sans Fil, the hospital for the adults where I would be working. Sans Fil once belonged to the Jesuits until the government exiled them for fomenting insurrection. It is a large, bleak, white two-story building which houses men on the first floor and women on the second. Each floor consists of two rooms, one for tuberculosis patients and the other for those with other chronic diseases. A large patio attached to the façade at a right angle serves as a place to distribute food so those waiting do not have to stand in the sun.

Here are housed the poorest of the poor – the forgotten, the neglected, the abused. They have no home, no family, and no representation. Many have been found lying in the streets; others were involved in automobile accidents and could not pay for care. Some were refused admission to a hospital and just left to die. Of the 150 human beings here, most are nursed back to health, but many die. Some just need a bath and food but others have tuberculosis, diarrhea and a variety of tropical diseases.

An impending gloom hangs over the place. There is a stench that is a combination of human excrement and disinfectant. Cachectic men in green scrub suits lie on the small concrete porch, lazily swatting attacking flies. Inside are rows of metal bed frames, each with a rotting mattress and vinyl sheets. Underneath are soiled plastic bedpans and urinals. Those with intractable coughs also have cuspidors. As I walk in, to my left is a contorted but smiling young man with a pink rosary around his neck, quadriplegic from polio. Several men are dying. They have no muscle mass, just sagging flesh attached to bone. Their cheeks are hollow with stubble of an unshaven beard sticking out of their pale, black faces. Their heads look like skulls, as if they have already begun to decompose. They have no energy to swat the multitude of flies that crawl on them with impunity. Others lie asleep with their genitals exposed revealing an ulcerated penis or swollen groin glands, the result of neglected venereal disease. Overlooking the rooms are pictures of Jesus Christ. As He gazes at this, He is probably glad that someone is caring for "the least of My brethen," but He also realizes that His message of 2000 years ago has been greatly distorted in this country whose official religion is Roman Catholic.

Still reeling from culture shock, I was taken by Fr. Demers on a visit to the palatial home of an elite family. The Pierres live in Pétionville, a suburb of Port-au-Prince which has the highest density of millionaires in the Caribbean.

The Pierre's house is set back amidst a well-cultivated arboretum, complete with a palm-treed lined driveway and manicured flower-bed encircling a spacious stone patio. A Mercedes, a 1930's roadster and assorted sports cars clutter the driveway. The house is even more ostentatious. It is split level with an inlaid marble floor covered with Persian rugs. The posh furniture is complemented by Cubist paintings, all crowned by an ornate crystal chandelier.

Mr. Pierre, a well-built balding man in his fifties, greeted me. Fashionably attired in a blue leisure suit and with gold chains intertwined among the thick gray hair of his exposed chest, he looked like the owner of a pornographic magazine. His wife, a svelte woman of 45, was stunning in her full-length azure dress. They are mulattos, the 2% of Haiti which has retained economic power for generations, no matter who has ruled.

Gracious hosts, the Pierres deferred to my ignorance and prevented the conversation from lapsing into French, Haiti's official language until 1987. Only a small percentage of the Haitians actually speak it. To the vast majority, Creole is the only language. During my stay in Haiti, most Haitians I met could not speak French, but I never met one who could not speak Creole. It was formed by the slaves who combined their African tongues with Norman French. Initially, Creole seems limited with its simple grammar and small vocabulary, but one can express most of the nuances of English with it; moreover, imaginative words have recently been created. For example, the word for copy is "zewòk"' razor is "jilèt" and penile erection is "pinokyo."

The existence of the Creole language is an insult to Mr. Pierre. He considers it to be disrespectful if his children speak it in his presence. Creole represents a bastardization of French and therefore of French culture, the measure of status to the elite. To the masses, Creole is a source of pride and there is continual conflict whether French or Creole should be taught in the school. This proverb personifies the struggle:

> Pale franse pa di lespri pou sa.
> Just speaking French doesn't mean one can think.

Between sips of chablis, Mr. Pierre told me about himself. His elite status is assured by a family-controlled franchise on pharmaceuticals imported to Haiti; however, he was bored with this sinecure and preferred to discuss his social life—his donations to the Michèle Duvalier Foundation, the latest society ball and his recent trip to Paris. Mr. Pierre buys his clothes in New York but his shoes in Paris. With unabashed pretentiousness, he explained in fluent English that unlike the nouveaux riches, he never paid full price when shopping. Old money gives one influential connections.

He had no interest whatsoever in the plight of the poor. Lazy, listless and without ambition, they deserved their fate. They were born to serve. He resented American meddling. We had no business complaining about human rights abuses or rigged elections. Haiti needed no external interferences, and he proudly told me of how Papa Doc rebuffed an American ambassador who had tried to dictate Haitian policy. He felt that political repression could continue with impunity because of Haiti's proximity to Cuba and the questionable status of an American military base in Guantanamo Bay whose lease expires in 1999.

Mr. Pierre is typical of the elite. Superficially, they are likeable, always thanking me for helping their poor countrymen, inviting me to dinner and speaking of progress in Haiti. Beneath this genteel veneer, they are devoid of compassion. They live a life of leisure, decadence and social posturing. Cultured, multilingual and well-mannered, they have no intention of bucking the system that protects their pococurante existence. They receive their education in Paris or the United States and spend their summers on Haiti's beautiful beaches. One wealthy Haitian, when I queried why more was not being done to help the poor responded, "That's what you're here for."

The deep dichotomy in Haitian society is well-entrenched in its history. In one form or another, there have always been masters and slaves. The peasant was never paid fairly, whether a slave to French overlords or a laborer under the black and mulatto elites.

The island of Hispaniola was first colonized by the Spanish whose forced labor made short work of the native Indians. Consequently, a new labor force was found – Africans. The opportunistic French also claimed territory on Hispaniola and in the late seventeenth century, Spain ceded possession of the western third of the island to France. Thus was formed Haiti.

With its tropical climate and fertile soil, anything grew. Sugar, coffee, cotton, bananas, sisal and indigo all made Haiti more productive than the entire English thirteen colonies. However, the slave owners presided with unprecedented brutality. The slaves, many being members of warrior tribes, were not docile. They did not wait for the raising of the white man's consciousness and their frequent revolts were suppressed with a sadistic barbarism that could neither be forgotten, nor forgiven. Perpetrators were buried with only their honey-covered faces and genitals exposed and left to die amid feasting ants. Others were publicly blown apart by gunpowder packed in their rectums. The owners took the most desirable women, forming a third class – the mulattos.

The blacks, whites and the mulattos engaged in a complex political and military struggle that culminated in Haiti's becoming the first black republic. Two men dominated the action – Toussaint L'Ouverture and Jean-Jacques Dessalines. Inspiring a fanatical devotion that bordered on deification, these former slaves commanded the guerrilla warfare that vanquished the superiorly-armed French. While the French defeat is often ascribed to disease, they were actually outsmarted by the Haitian generals as their colonial forays into other tropical climates had been successful. L'Ouverture and Dessalines actually planned biological warfare, burning their own towns and retreating, waiting to mount their offensive during the rainy seasons – when malaria, typhoid and yellow fever would decimate the ill-equipped Caucasian immune system. Thus ended Napoleon's dream of conquering North America. Without a base to protect the Louisiana Territory, he was forced to sell it to the nascent United States.

By feigning a peace conference, the French captured L'Ouverture and during his confinement, he died. Dessalines did not succumb to the French platitudes, knowing their main goal was to restore the slavery that still existed on Martinique and Guadeloupe. He offered amnesty to all whites in Haiti. When they came out of hiding, they were massacred – all 20,000 of them – forever ridding Haiti of the specter of slavery. Grabbing the French tricolor flag, he ripped out the white middle, forming Haiti's flag and proclaiming the Republic in 1804.

What remained was a war-ravaged Haiti, isolated from the international community and with no economic infrastructure. Only the mulattos were left to communicate with the outside world and to revitalize Haiti. It never happened. The black military elite and mulattos fought for the prime land. Meanwhile, the peasant continued to be exploited. Forced labor was reinstituted, so many escaped to the countryside, becoming squatters. They just wanted to be left alone: to practice their religion, raise their families and enjoy life.

During the subsequent century, internecine political infighting stunted economic growth. Foreign business recolonized Haiti, controlling its banks and commerce while raping its treasury with false indemnities. When the Haitians objected, the gunboats arrived. The effete governments were unable to prevent rioting, looting and open warfare. Anarchy prevailed. In 1915, the U.S. Marines landed. While they were ostensibly to restore order, their real job was to protect American business interests while preventing the Germans, who also had interests in Haiti, from establishing a military base.

The Americans ended the chaos and built schools, roads and hospitals; however, a bloated bureaucracy sapped the treasury. Favoritism towards the mulattos encouraged resentment. More important, the Haitians were stripped of their dignity. The proud people who shattered the yoke of slavery were forced to tolerate Southern rednecks that refused to shake their hands. These interlopers displayed a disdain for Haitian culture, refusing to learn either Creole or French. Terrorist attacks by a peasant underground – the Cacos – along with eloquent protests from the elite forced an American withdrawal. By 1934, the military presence ended with the hope that Haiti could establish representative government.

It never happened. The mulatto and black elite, previously united in their assault on American occupation, soon returned to their senseless squabbling. The roads decayed, the plumbing rotted and the telephones stopped working. Within two decades, Haiti was again in anarchy. In 1956 and 1957, there were six presidents, all trying to appease a greedy elite and power-hungry military. It was an impossible and uncontrollable situation.

In 1957, a country doctor and leader of the emerging black middle class was elected President. François Duvalier was considered dull and pliable by both supporters and opponents. He tolerated insults to his face, always smiling and laughing them off. Haiti's power brokers had another pawn that would obsequiously patronize them.

Behind his mindless smile however, Duvalier plotted his ascendancy. Having been in a former President's cabinet, he knew that vacillation and appeasement only sealed one's doom. He understood that to have power in Haiti one had to balance the military. Thus were created the Tonton Macoutes, his secret police. They were from his constituency and received no official salary, only what they could extort, confiscate or steal.

A strange thing began to happen. Duvalier's opponents simply disappeared. Before the elite had realized what had happened, Duvalier was untouchable. The Tonton Macoutes terrorized the country, sneaking into people's homes at night, killing them and disposing of their bodies. The prisons swelled and torture became commonplace. The affable smile turned to an icy stare, and Duvalier tormented his supporters as much as his opponents, threatening a pile of bodies "as high as the Himalayas." Duvalier or "Papa Doc" then declared himself President-for-Life.

Although he survived coup attempts and American backed invasions, Papa Doc encountered one enemy he could not vanquish – heart failure. In 1971 he succumbed, but not before naming a successor, his 19-year-old son, Jean-Claude Duvalier. During Papa Doc's reign of terror, foreign investment dwindled, tourism stopped and many elite and middle-class professionals emigrated. Haiti now had political stability but its economy disintegrated. "Baby Doc" relaxed his father's repression: the Tonton Macoutes started beating people, rather than killing them. Tourism blossomed and the foreign investments returned. Baby Doc married a beautiful mulatto divorcee, Michèle Bennett, uniting the warring black bureaucracy and military with the mulatto elite. Michèle was Haiti's version of Evita Peron. Haiti with its industrious work force, political stability and pleasant climate was poised to become the Taiwan of the Caribbean.

Unfortunately, the bureaucrats and investors only helped themselves, taking advantage of industrious peasants. Cheap labor was used to produce export items rather than develop an economy that would sustain a steady growth. The most fertile area, the Artibonite Valley, was partially flooded to provide hydroelectric power to foreign investors, robbing many peasants of their agrarian livelihood.

On paper, economic growth appeared. During the 1970's, Haiti's gross national product rose annually. Unfortunately, 50% of the income went to less than 1% of the population. Meanwhile, the vast majority were making less than $140 per year. The poor were heavily taxed for their products, forcing them to sell at low prices to the tax-exempt politically powerful. Corporations who had their markets overseas were not concerned as they were still making a profit.

During this time, an ominous condition was developing. The population of Haiti doubled in only 30 years. In order to feed themselves, the peasants cultivated the mountains, cutting down the trees that protected the soil. Now most of Haiti's topsoil has been forever lost to the rivers that become mud with each rainfall. Many peasants moved into the cities, especially into Port-au-Prince where unemployment is at least 50%. Since many were starving and ill, the international community increased aid to Haiti via direct grants and bank loans. Most of it simply vanished. Canada, when twenty million dollars of its aid was stolen, refused to send more, dubbing Haiti a "kleptocracy."

The International Monetary Fund (IMF) reluctantly agreed to continue loans to Haiti, but stipulated that the money be monitored by its representative, Marc Bazin. A native Haitian, Bazin quickly spotted accounting irregularities as money was transferred among Haiti's financial institutions. There was no apparent attempt to hide the theft in taxes or finance charges; the money was simply stolen. Bazin also suggested that export taxes be paid equally by all. In Haiti, he who controls the export taxes controls the country. High taxes force the peasant to sell their products, especially coffee, to political cronies who are naturally tax-exempt. Within five months, Bazin was ejected from

Haiti. All warring factions agreed not to tolerate anyone who hindered their graft.

Private organizations working in Haiti also encountered financial difficulties. The government insisted that all money be placed in the Bank of Haiti. This hoarding of American dollars has allowed Haiti to print on its currency "five gourdes equal one dollar" since 1919, making the gourde impervious to the vicissitudes of international exchange. Many organizations refused and instead increased importing material goods. The Haitian government was not to be outsmarted. It simply assessed the value of the food and put a huge tax on it. It is now routine for food, farming equipment and medical supplies to sit in customs for years until the proper entry taxes are paid. The Ethiopian government used the same technique with great success to fill its coffers. Food being shipped to feed the starving was outrageously taxed and the guilt-ridden industrial world anted up.

In the early 1980's, Haiti was pummeled by forces beyond its control. Since it was dependent on export income, the world recession diminished the industrialized world's interest in Haiti's products. Hurricanes destroyed its cash crops, especially coffee, considered in some circles to be the best in the world.

Haiti's tourist industry had been foundering since the mid-seventies. The beggars of Port-au-Prince constantly harassed vacationers. The cruise ships started to bypass Haiti and continued directly to Jamaica. However, it was a report from the Center of Disease Control in Atlanta that was the death knell. It described a new disease, Acquired Immune Deficiency Syndrome or AIDS, and cited four high risk groups – homosexuals, hemophiliacs, drug addicts, and Haitians. As the hysteria increased, tourism came to a standstill. The hotels emptied, the roulette wheels stopped and the boutiques closed down. Haitians were eventually removed from the high-risk category, but the damage had already been done. Now only missionaries and idealists visit. Haiti has sunk from pessimism to frank despair.

There are simply no jobs. Even foreign investors, spurred by a $3.00 daily minimum wage, provide jobs for only 6% of the work force. Men are sold by the government at $3.00 a head to the neighboring Dominican Republic to cut the sugarcane crop. No one else is willing to swing a machete for ten hours in 100-degree heat for $1.50 a day. From this meager wage, they must pay for room and board – shanties and crumbs. The owners munificently extend credit, so that after three months of hard work many laborers actually owe money. Those who complain are beaten. This indentured slavery filled the coffers of the American-based multinational corporation that owned the sugarcane fields until the late 1980's, Gulf + Western.

Although patriotic, the Haitians are desperate. They are willing to risk anything, including their lives, to leave. Those who could have built a new Haiti, the incipient middle class, have fled and live in France, Canada and the United States. Entire families pool their resources so that one member can emigrate. They must endure endless lines, hassles with bureaucracy and thievery by travel agents. But in the end, they are rewarded. Haitians quickly achieve a life in the United States they could never dream of in Haiti. With the money they send back, more family members are able to emigrate.

For most of the poor though, obtaining a passport, visa and airline ticket is a distant dream. Those who decide to leave jam onto dilapidated boats and begin a dangerous odyssey north. As one Haitian put it, "The teeth of the shark are sweeter than Duvalier's hell." The boat leaves at night and twelve hours later arrives at a beach where scantily-clad whites are wind surfing and playing volleyball. They have finally arrived in America, the land of opportunity. Triumphantly disembarking, they soon encounter blacks who – strangely – speak Creole. Then comes the shocking realization: after saving their money for two years, they have been deposited at Haiti's Club Med.

Even those who are on course have no guarantees. Their boats, wooden platforms with makeshift sails, frequently capsize, making headlines in Miami when their bodies wash up on the beach. Others are preyed upon by Cuban pirates. Also, the smugglers overload a boat to maximize profits, then randomly throw people overboard.

Those who miraculously arrive, sun-stroked and dehydrated, are not greeted with open arms. They are immediately placed in detention centers where they languish in legal limbo until the courts decide their fate. The American government argues that they are fleeing poverty and not repression and should not be granted political asylum; however, since the Haitian government considers fleeing the country to be treason, those returned are often beaten and imprisoned. Because Haiti is not a Communist country, most courts have refused to release detained Haitians. Some have become so depressed that they commit suicide, something they rarely do in their own country. To prevent further court battles, the Coast Guard began to patrol international waters to seize fleeing Haitians so they can be returned to Haiti without due process.

In spite of these numerous obstacles, there are almost 1,000,000 Haitians living in the United States. Many arrived illiterate, penniless and unable to speak English. They suffered discrimination, culture shock, and imprisonment. The AIDS hysteria has made them pariahs. Since many are illegal aliens, employers exploit them, paying them much less than the minimum wage and denying benefits. Security deposits are not refunded on apartments. Nonetheless, they remain surprisingly optimistic.

Most Haitians learn English within six months. Education is revered and 90% of teenage Haitians attend high school. They do not have the 9 to 5 concept and are willing to work long hours. Violent crime against non-Haitians is virtually unheard of. The percentage of those on public assistance is no higher than that of the general population. The Haitians, while keeping a low profile, have proven they can do well if only given a chance.

The Duvalier government had no intention of giving native Haitians a chance. While Michèle Duvalier created an overly air-conditioned room so that the elite women could wear furs to parties, the government controlled the bleak situation by censorship, intimidation and torture. Every morning, the propaganda trucks rode through Port-au-Prince, stroking national pride by reminding them of their conquest over slavery. The Tonton Macoutes, now renamed the Volunteers for National Security, pervaded all aspects of life, quelling dissent. Attempts by laborers to unionize were quickly crushed.

Nonetheless, the writing was on the wall. The situation was intolerable and simply could not last. Sporadic rebellions began. In 1984, food riots started in Gonaives, a city in Central Haiti. While many were so hungry they were killing their dogs, a warehouse filled with food donated by CARE was locked. Local government officials were demanding payment for it. When opposition formed, the Tonton Macoutes killed the leader and beat his pregnant wife. The ensuing outrage overwhelmed local authorities and Duvalier dispatched the army, that quickly quelled the riots with characteristic savagery. Nobody ever received any food.

Organized dissent began also, most of it led by the Catholic Church. This was a reversal of its previous role in which it formed a alliance with the oligarchy and the military. Until recently, all major clerical appointments from the Vatican had to receive government approval. This medieval arrangement bonded the church and state politically. To this day, prominent church officials live in huge mansions with guard dogs, and the elite send their children to the best Catholic prep schools.

With Vatican II, Catholicism began to appeal more to the masses. It had always been the official religion, but the religion of the people is Voodoo, an African creed in which spirits or "loas" pervade every aspect of life. The ceremonies, with their lascivious dances, spiritual possession and decapitated chickens make it a "must" for tourists. However these displays mask a complex religion that is poorly understood by non-Haitians. The "oungans" or priests are articulate and educated community leaders who do not try to compete with Catholicism, but wisely incorporate it.

The Latin mass with its little action bored the peasants; however, with Vatican II, the people could use the vernacular Creole, dance and play bongo drums. With this increased bond to the people, the church became their advocate.

Radio Soleil, the Catholic radio station, politely derided the government; however, it was the Pope's visit in 1983 that increased Church activism. In front of tens of thousands of people, with Duvalier beside him, the Pope spoke forcefully about "the deep need for justice" in Haitian society. Unlike his approach in Central America, the Pope's policy endorsed clerical militancy in Haiti. His very presence was contingent upon the repeal of the policy of government approval for prominent Church positions. The newspapers were censored, so the Pope's speech was never published. Mr. Bennett, President Duvalier's father-in-law, wrote a scathing rebuttal implying a possible repeat of the assassination of Archbishop Romero in El Salvador if clerical opposition continued. Nonetheless, as a violent response to conscientious clerics invites the reproach of the industrialized world, the Haitian government was gradually being forced into tolerating open disagreement from the clergy, whether they liked it or not.

While Haiti paid lip service to American overtures about democracy, their elections were a sham. When Baby Doc ran for reelection for President-for-Life in 1985, he received 1,300,000 votes. There was one dissenter. Elections to the fifty-nine member National Assembly were equally farcical. Serious opposition candidates were not permitted on the ballot. Even so, since the President had veto power over this rubber-stamp parliament, elections were academic. Haiti, truly, had a one-man, one-vote system. The President was the only one who voted; and his word was law. Democracy was simply a game, the prize being American dollars.

Though it appeared that Haiti's totalitarian government at least provided political stability, it was the mass exodus of the up-and-coming that had prevented violent revolution. The Dominican Republic, the Bahamas, Quebec, France and especially the United States acted as a safety valve. Only Port-au-Prince has more Haitians than New York City and the third largest concentration is in Miami.

When it became more difficult for Haitians to enter the United States, the safety valve was plugged. Even recent medical school graduates could not find American residencies and the Haitian government was forced to decrease its medical school enrollment by 50%. Not only the poor, but now the up-and-coming had no place to go. Early in 1986, the riots started again, with a renewed vigor that even the random butchery of the Tonton Macoutes could not stop. The government closed Radio Soleil and two other church stations but soon rumors abounded that the fall of the Duvalier dynasty was imminent.

Jean-Claude Duvalier, to prove he was in control, drove through Port-au-Prince in his Mercedes and proclaimed his authority "was as firmly attached as a monkey's tail." Meanwhile, Haitian diplomats—protected from searches by international law—absconded from Haiti with suitcases full of money. Several days later the Duvalier family and several political cronies boarded an American military jet destined for France. The same man who six months prior had received over 99% of the vote escaped with an estimated fortune of half-a-billion dollars. The Duvalier dynasty had ended.

While Jean-Claude was complaining in his four-star French hotel that he could not get lobster for breakfast, the cumulative rage of almost three decades of repression spilled onto the streets of Haiti. Members of the Tonton Macoutes were killed and dismembered while their houses burned. Shops were looted and the large mausoleum of Papa Doc was desecrated. Only the foresight of Jean-Claude in taking his father's remains prevented their being scattered on the streets of Port-au-Prince. The posters of Jean-Claude with his Gucci-laden wife that littered public places were torn down and urinated upon.

Haiti is now governed by a junta of military and civilian leaders who are promising democratic elections. Some pundits are optimistic, while others see the departure of Duvalier as symbolic with no concomitant change in the underlying political structure that has for generations resulted in gross inequities in Haitian society. Only time will tell if representative government and justice can prevail.

Chapter 2

The Clinics: Becoming an Old Time Doctor

Lasante se pi gwo richès
Health is the greatest of riches.

Haitian proverb

As a medical student, I spent time with the general practitioner who delivered me. Dr. Donald Sharbaugh was a dying breed. In his forty years of practice, he had done everything: neonatology, orthopedic surgery, gynecology—along with the usual care of sore throats, strained backs and high blood pressure. As is typical of his vintage, he had little use for modern medicine and referred to it as "CYA" or "cover-your-ass" medicine. He resented the intrusion of government, lawyers, and high technology into his domain. However, he realized his era was passing and perhaps felt it was a good thing, although he never admitted it.

Dr. Sharbaugh told me that medicine is nothing but a battle of wits between you and the patient. Observation is key. You must begin examining the patient as soon as you lay eyes on him—his gait as he walks into the room, how he shakes your hand, his facial expressions as he describes his problem. To him, medicine is an art, not a science.

Although many would agree with Dr. Sharbaugh's philosophy, few actually practice it. Spurred by the public's demand for technology, legal considerations and a seemingly infinite supply of money, American physicians are forced to practice high-tech defensive medicine, where objective data are revered and instinct and judgment are secondary. If the patient has a headache, get a CAT scan. If he has chest pain, do a cardiac catheterization.

Dr. Sharbaugh's generation laments this trend but nonetheless it is the wave of the future. It is leading to a cold, dehumanizing brand of medicine, but more correct diagnoses are made earlier so that rapid treatment can be initiated. Frequently though, technological facts and all the tests are negative. It is then concluded that the symptoms are "psychosomatic" – a diplomatic way of suggesting the patient may be crazy. This is preferable to admitting that medicine is still in a state of abysmal ignorance, immobilized by the immune system, baffled by the brain, and confounded by the common cold. Medicine is still an art, not a science.

In Haiti, medicine is truly an art. It was just me with my stethoscope, and the patient, both sitting on hard wooden chairs. My decisions were based on observation, instinct, and a few simple laboratory tests. If I thought treatment was warranted, I gave it. Those who were dying. I just tried to comfort. If I was unsure, I still had to make a decision; there was no one else to ask. There were no bureaucrats harassing me with meaningless paperwork. There was no malpractice to worry about. It was real medicine in its primitive form. Dr. Sharbaugh would have loved it.

At first, when I began working in the clinics, I felt woefully inadequate. In front of me were dozens of Haitians, speaking a language I could not speak, from a culture I did not understand, and with diseases I had never seen.

I learned quickly. I had no choice. The tropical diseases that had been textbook abstractions were now three-dimensional reality. Soon I was able to treat the common problems – tuberculosis, malaria, typhoid, and others. Slowly but surely, the rapid blur of guttural syllables emanating from their mouths began to make sense. Within several months, I was conversant in Creole.

Also, I had to learn physical diagnosis, or proper examination of the patient. In medical school, careful examination of the patient is stressed. In reality, it never happens. It has been replaced by CAT scans, ultrasounds, and nuclear imaging. Since these were not available to me, my physical diagnosis book became my Bible. I had to listen carefully to the lungs, inching my stethoscope across the front and back of the chest trying to hear a wheeze that would add to my suspicion of tuberculosis. When I examined the abdomen, my fingers probed under the ribs and pelvic bones searching for an enlarged organ. While doing this, I watched the patient's face for the slight grimace that signaled tenderness or discomfort.

Having acquired these new skills and knowledge, I still faced another problem. Haitians frequently lie about their symptoms. This changed the rules completely. I could no longer rely on the cornerstone of medicine, the patient's history. It is the history – what the patient tells you is the problem – where 80% of the diagnoses are made. Physical exam and laboratory tests are only confirmatory. In the United States, other than in workers compensation cases, physicians hear the truth as it is perceived by the patient. If a man complains of chest pain, it exists. He may exaggerate it, perhaps tailoring his symptoms to the latest Reader's Digest article, but he wants to receive the best possible care and therefore gives an accurate assessment of his problem.

In Haiti, it is different. Port-au-Prince is replete with social-welfare organizations dispensing free food and medicine. In a country with massive unemployment, many make their livelihood shopping place to place with the same story. If they can obtain a surplus of medicine or food, they sell it. You can not blame them. They are just trying to survive.

It was truly a battle of wits between me and the patient. Often, a patient would complain of abdominal pain. I would ask the usual array of questions; do you have fevers, diarrhea or painful urination. They would respond yes to every one. When I examined them, I found nothing wrong and told them so. Then the truth would come out. They would ask me for food, often telling me they were good Catholics. This only strengthened my resolve not to give anything. I would reply, "M' doktè, m' pa Papa Nowèl" , " I'm a doctor, not Santa Claus." I had to balance compassion with firmness so the neediest got help.

It was especially disheartening when parents would use their sick children to get charity. It was even possible to rent pathetic, starving children either to take to the clinics or to use for begging on the streets.

One woman brought me her thirteen-year-old daughter. The child was wearing a tattered sleeveless drab red dress and weighed 55 pounds. She had a cough and fever and this, combined with her listless emaciated appearance, made me quickly conclude she had tuberculosis. I gave the mother the medicine for her and told them to return weekly to renew it. After finishing work for the morning, I went to have lunch with a friend who worked for the Salvation Army. During our conversation, I described the plight of this family. Barbara, a handsome Swiss woman of 35, had a quick flash of anger in her eyes. She had seem them today, too. The mother had been bringing the daughter to the Salvation Army for the past year. Barbara suspected that the mother was selling the medicine rather than giving it to the daughter. She had 12 other children and no husband. When this child dies, the mother will shop with one of her other children.

The vast majority of patients I saw needed help and needed it desperately. Illiterate, broke, and without marketable skills, they had no hope of advancement. They needed to eat, to sleep, and had no way of obtaining money to do so. They were sentenced to a living hell where their very existence depended upon the charity of others.

Health care is available from the Hôpital Général, located in central Port-au-Prince. Although a consultation is free, everything else must be paid for including linen, food, medicine, syringes and lab tests. If surgery is needed, the patients even have to purchase the gloves, drapes and required instruments. This seems reasonable until one sees the prices – $1.60 for an intravenous needle, $50.00 for antibiotics, $20.00 for laboratory tests. Many Americans could not afford these prices. Many of these supplies are donated by industrialized nations to be distributed to the needy for free or minimal cost. The poor Haitians, ignorant and gullible, sink their meager life savings into health care without being cured.

One problem I didn't anticipate was huge ulcers that refused to heal. They occurred everywhere but most frequently were on the legs. One man had an ulcer that involved half of his lower leg, extending from the knee to the ankle. Just looking at the ulcer turned even my hardened stomach. His black skin yielded to an ugly brick red wound with ragged edges. It had rugged contours – mountains and abysses of glistening raw meat – giving it a refractile appearance. Through the abysses filled with yellow pus coursed purple veins. In the middle of the wound, the underlying bone peeked through. It reminded me of a dissection from anatomy class. The patient swatted at the flies constantly lighting upon the wound using the crucifix of his rosary.

Wounds such as this start from small cuts that refuse to heal. In the industrialized world, small cuts heal quickly because a well-nourished body has a functioning immune system to prevent infections and the capacity to manufacture extra tissues needed for wound healing. In those who are malnourished, the body can not spare the extra energy, since it is too busy maintaining basic metabolic processes. Consequently, these wounds continue to grow. The Haitians are unable to afford shoes and walk in raw sewage, so the wound gets infected and reinfected until it becomes unmanageable. Sickeningly often, only an amputation can prevent the infection from spreading.

In spite of some frustrating diseases, working in the clinics was where I saved the most lives. The biggest killer in Haiti is diarrhea and is the main reason why a large percentage of children die before age five. In the industrialized world, diarrhea is usually caused by bacterial and viral infections, but in Haiti worms and protozoa also precipitate this condition. These infections prevent the intestine from absorbing water so that it passes through rapidly, resulting in diarrhea.

Diarrhea can be caused not only by infections, but also by malabsorption. The biggest culprit in Haiti is artificial milk preparations with lactose, a complex sugar that cannot be absorbed unless it is broken down by the enzyme lactase. Cow's milk contains lactose, so that Caucasians, who have been weaned on cow's milk since the Middle Ages, have been selected out so that almost all have lactase. Unfortunately, many blacks—as many as 30%—lack it and will develop diarrhea when given milk preparations that are distributed by altruistic organizations, sold in stores and even advertised on television.

The best milk for babies is breast milk. Cow's milk is for cows; people's milk is for people. Over millions of years of evolution, breast milk has been refined to the perfect food, containing all the essential vitamins, minerals, and immunoglobulins to protect against diarrhea. Nursing mothers have been encouraged to supplement their babies' diet with assorted concoctions, but it is not necessary; breast milk has everything. Breast-feeding also serves as nature's method of birth-control because nursing mothers ovulate less frequently. Since breast-feeding is not foolproof, American physicians never advocate it for simply this reason.

Unfortunately, many Haitian women do not breast-feed, either because they have food to give the baby, or because they themselves are too malnourished to produce milk. Another problem is that breast-feeding has been discouraged by American business interests. In the 1950's, it was fashionable for American mothers to bottle-feed, providing a huge market for artificial milk. With increasing evidence that breast milk was better not only for the babies' health but also for mother-infant bonding, breast-feeding once again became the vogue. Since the milk producers had a shrinking market, they looked to other countries. Free artificial milk was distributed to naive women in Third-World countries for their babies. It lasted about two or three weeks, just long enough for the mother's own milk to dry up. They were forced to obtain the artificial milk again. Needless to say, it was no longer free. This practice was stopped after an acrimonious boycott of the Nestle corporation, one of the milk producers. However, the damage was done. Up-and-coming women in Third-World countries prefer to bottle-feed and their babies get diarrhea more often.

Diarrhea is lethal, not because of the infections that precipitate it, but from the dehydration. Without fluid, oxygen cannot be transported to the vital organs such as the heart. This results in the heart contracting less effectively, so that the fluid is pumped even slower – a vicious circle. The blood pressure drops, the child goes into shock and dies. To prevent this, the fluid must be replaced.

Before doing this, I had to immediately identify the dehydrated babies. Jean was typical. His pathetic mother was attired in a filthy gray rag that could not hide her frail 70-pound frame. She held Jean up to me, not saying anything, as if her son's problem were obvious. She was right.

Jean eyed me suspiciously. As his mouth was slightly agape, I could see his parched tongue behind his dry lips. His dark brown eyes were sunk deep into his head but alertly followed my every move. This was enough to diagnosis dehydration.

I undressed him, unwrapping the tight cloth that swaddled his torso. He responded by howling, tears rolling down his concave cheeks, thrashing his liberated stick-like arms and legs wildly as I invaded his personal space. This made me optimistic, first because he could make tears – something severely dehydrated babies can not do – and secondly because he fought back. Babies who passively accept the poking and prodding of total strangers are quite sick.

My hand instinctively felt the soft spot or fontanelle on the top of his head. It is the rhomboid indentation formed by the skull bones before they grow together during childhood. Through it one can feel the cerebral spinal fluid which bathes the brain. When a child becomes dehydrated, the level of cerebral spinal fluid decreases and the soft spot sinks. Mothers of all cultures know this is a danger sign. In the United States, they take the baby to the hospital. In Haiti, they turn the baby upside-down.

I felt a depressed soft spot in Jean, even though he was crying. Then I gently pinched the skin over his chest. Instead of snapping back quickly, it slowly flattened, like a tent whose main supports have been pulled out – another sign of dehydration. I listened to his lungs and heart in-between howls, noting that they both sounded normal but that the heart was beating rapidly, a compensatory mechanism for fluid loss.

I asked the mother, "Li gen dyare?" "Does he have diarrhea?"

"Wi," she replied, "e lafyèv tou." "Yes, and fever too."

"Ou ba li tete ou?" "Do you breast-feed him?"

"No, m' pa gen lèt," she said with her head dropping. "No, I don't have milk."

Jean was moderately dehydrated, and in the United States would immediately be admitted to a hospital. Unfortunately, on a typical clinic day, there were twenty babies like Jean. Since it was not practical to hospitalize them all, I taught the mothers to rehydrate them orally. A child with diarrhea can not simply be given water because electrolytes – sodium, potassium and chloride – are also lost and they must be replaced. The body has infinitely complex biochemical processes to maintain these electrolytes at constant concentration, as they are vital for basic functions. For example, a slight change in the potassium concentration can result in abnormal heart beats, muscle weakness, and in extreme cases, paralysis.

I would give the mothers packets of electrolyte powder to be mixed with water. I had to explain how to make the solution and then have them repeat the directions until I was satisfied they understood. It was difficult until I learned Creole. When it was first discovered that babies could be rehydrated by this method, only electrolytes were put in the packets. Then it was noticed that by adding glucose, a simple sugar, the solution was absorbed with greater efficiency in the intestine. This discovery has saved more lives than all the cancer research combined. Oral rehydration is used extensively throughout the Third

World in an effort to decrease the 5,000,000 deaths caused annually by diarrhea and dehydration.

At first, I had difficulty telling the mothers how much to add to a packet. I would say, "a liter," but they had no idea what I was talking about. Finally, I found a government pamphlet on oral rehydration that was written in Creole. Since few poor Haitians can read, it did them no good but it certainly helped me. The Haitians drink a cheap local cola that is made of fruit juice and an ungodly amount of sugar that only a Haitian can tolerate. This pamphlet said that three of these cola bottles equal one liter. I would tell them to pour three cola bottles of water in a pot and boil it, for sterilization. Allow it to cool and then add a packet of electrolyte powder and stir. Every time the baby had diarrhea, they were to give it a cup of the solution.

Jean's mother understood the directions and repeated them perfectly. Not all the mothers did. One woman brought me her dehydrated six-month-old and after examining him, I took a packet of electrolyte powder and began explaining how to use it.

"First, place three cola bottles of water in a basin and boil it," I told her in my heavily-accented Creole.

"Then add one packet of the powder. Give the baby one cup of the solution every two hours and add a half cup every time he has diarrhea. Give the water slowly with a spoon so the baby doesn't vomit."

Satisfied, I asked her to repeat the directions for me. As she did so, in slow deliberate Creole, I beamed with self-pride. I was really saving a life. She then triumphantly concluded her rendition with, "Then put the baby in the basin for a bath."

Many lives were saved, at least temporarily, by this method. Another life-threatening problem I frequently dealt with was abscesses. An abscess is a collection of white blood cells that accumulate to fight an infection. As it grows, it can break into the bloodstream and spread to the liver, brain or kidneys. A widespread infection like this can be fatal. For this reason, an abscess must be drained and antibiotics given. The Haitians got them everywhere – on their heads, in their mouths, in the groin, and even in the rectum. They were painful and, if allowed to spread – fatal. After several months, I had drained every conceivable type.

A young woman, Magdeline, came to me complaining of low back pain and fevers. Back pain is the bane of American medicine because there are few known causes for it and even fewer cures. Fifty percent of American males present to their physician with back pain at least once in their life. Sometimes a cause such as a ruptured disc is found. More often, extensive testing reveals nothing and vague diagnoses such as muscle strain are given, resulting in frustration for both the physician and patient. Haitians get back and neck pain from carrying heavy objects such as sacks of charcoal and buckets of water on their heads.

This was not the case with Magdeline. She could barely walk and localized the pain to the left flank of her lower back. This area bulged when compared to the other side and felt hot. When I pressed on it, she screamed. If she had been white, I could easily have diagnosed the abscess because the skin would also be red, but in blacks I did not have this luxury. Nonetheless, I was certain she had an abscess.

Ideally, this abscess should be drained painlessly and with sterile technique in an operating room. I did my best to simulate one in spite of the flies buzzing around. I had Magdeline lie prone on a wooden table and gathered the equipment I needed: gloves, iodine, anesthesia, gauze, alcohol, and a scalpel. I scrubbed her skin with iodine and saline until it was a smooth glistening ebony and injected lidocaine, a local anesthetic into the area I planned to cut. Quickly, I plunged the scalpel in her skin. She felt nothing. The blade made a half-inch incision and as I pulled it out, a frothy, putrid, white pus suddenly jetted into the air like a geyser. When the pressure was relieved, the pus stopped but some still remained. After slightly lengthening the incision, I began to squeeze it out.

"Ooyyee," she screamed in the high-pitched ululation unique to Haitian women.

"Prèske fine", "Almost done," I said.

Anesthesia does not help when squeezing abscesses. The pus continued to exude with each squeeze until more than a cup had come out. Finally, after what seemed like an eternity to both of us, it stopped. Soaking some gauze in alcohol, I wrapped it into a cord and pushed it into the wound letting the end hang out into the air.

"Ooyyee," she yelled again. The alcohol stung.

This would allow the pus to drain and prevent the wound from closing before the infection was eradicated. She thanked me repeatedly, even though she found the procedure so uncomfortable. Haitians are an appreciative and polite people.

Magdeline also needed to be treated with Penicillin, preferably intravenously every four hours. This is the best route to ensure that the antibiotic gets to the infected area. However, I had to compromise and give one dose intramuscularly and the rest orally. Penicillin is no longer the best drug for abscesses. Thirty years ago it was, but some bacteria have developed resistance and require more expensive synthetic drugs unavailable in Haiti.

Magdeline did very well. The fevers stopped, the pain subsided, and soon she was walking comfortably. After a week I pulled the gauze out of her back as the pus had stopped draining. She even got a job carrying food to the patients at Sans Fil.

Sometimes, an abscess would not respond to Penicillin. One child, Marimath, had been abandoned at the clinics when I first saw her. Although her mother must have been heartbroken, for Marimath it was a stroke of good luck. The Missionaries of Charity would find her a loving home in the industrialized world. Sometimes I wondered if I was doing a child a favor by saving it and returning it to the same miserable environment that spawned its initial state – but saving those who were to be adopted was very satisfying.

Marimath was having fevers and cried constantly. Covering her bald, black head were little fluctuant mounds, all abscesses. They extended down the nape of her neck to her back. Otherwise, she appeared healthy.

I took her to the Children's Home and proceeded to lance the abscesses. Pus spewed out of each one as the scalpel blade incised the skin of each mound. Poor Marimath howled uncontrollably at what I hoped would prove to be justifiable torture. I wished I had the equipment to put her under general anesthesia. I started her on large doses of intravenous Penicillin but after three days, the high fever persisted and she refused to eat. Obviously, the Penicillin was not working.

I found a small amount of Methacillin but it was expired, meaning that its manufacturer no longer guaranteed its effectiveness. Methacillin is Penicillin with a slight modification in its chemical structure that enables it to kill types of bacteria that have evolved Penicillin resistance. I had no choice but to try it.

The results were miraculous. Within one day the pus quit draining and the fevers stopped, never to return. Marimath began to eat and gain weight. Soon she could sit, a huge smile displacing her chubby cheeks as she played with her toys. She is now being reared in Europe, making some couple very happy.

Actually, expired drugs are usually effective. For legal reasons, drug companies underestimate when a drug will lose its potency. Unsellable expired surpluses are then given to Third-World countries. Both parties benefit because the drug companies get a tax write-off and pose as altruistic while these poor countries receive medicine they could never afford.

This practice often put me in a quandary. There is nothing more frustrating than putting a patient on a medicine and not seeing a response. If the drug is not expired, then I could assume it was the wrong drug and start another. But what if the drug is expired? Is the patient not responding because I chose the wrong drug or because it is no longer effective? I never knew.

To help me choose the proper antibiotics, I set up a small laboratory. Armed with my microscope from medical school, an assortment of donated chemicals, slides, pipettes and test tubes, I became proficient at simple tests like the Gram stain. Invented over 100 years ago, it is still the mainstay of modern medicine to determine the initial antibiotic treatment of an infection. Because of the biochemical structure of the cell wall, the Gram stain colors some bacteria blue – Gram positive – while those that are Gram negative appear red. Also, the bacteria have different shape, either rods or spheres called cocci. This information along with the identification of the infection allows one to prescribe the proper antibiotic. For example, abscesses caused by Gram positive cocci often respond to Penicillin. On the other hand, infections caused by Gram negative rods need Gentamycin.

Another skill I was forced to learn was dentistry. Poor Bernadette, a young woman with tuberculosis and malnutrition, also had an abscess the size of a golf ball under her chin. I lanced it, draining ugly yellow pus. The Gram stain showed Gram positive cocci so I began treating her with Penicillin. However, two weeks later, the pus continued to pour out of the incision. Rather than start another antibiotic, I tried a novel approach – a more thorough examination of the patient.

My Bible, the physical diagnosis book, said that abscesses under the chin may be caused by tooth infections, so I looked in her mouth. It was a complete disaster. One-third of her teeth were missing and the remaining were decayed, eroded, and black. Some were so rotten they had split, each fragment being in a different direction. Two were intact but loose, swimming in a pool of pus encased by necrotic gums – the source of the abscess. As I gazed at this mess, a putrid stench bludgeoned me.

Haitians have pitiful dental hygiene. The entire country is addicted to sugar. Babies are weaned on sugar water and spend their childhood sucking on the cheap and abundant sugarcane, their main source of calories. A Haitian can not even drink a glass of orange juice without five tablespoons of sugar. There is no strong movement to fluoridate the water. All these factors combined to make Haiti a dentist's nightmare.

Anyone who has had an abscessed tooth knows the pain is excruciating, like a jackhammer pounding on the jaw, sending reverberations through the skull. Yet Bernadette, like many Haitians, learned to live with it, just as migraine patients become inured to their headaches. I was going to extract her teeth myself with a pair of pliers, but, fortunately for Bernadette, a dentist from Connecticut was visiting. Dr. Jerry Lowney was a ruddy Irishman of 50 who continued his daily five-mile run in Port-au-Prince in spite of 100-degree temperature, devastating humidity, exhaust fumes from thousands of cars without mufflers, and steep hills. He deftly extracted Bernadette's abscessed teeth, earning her eternal gratitude. Within days the pus stopped draining and, a week later, the abscess was gone.

Jerry's impromptu dental clinic was the first thing I had seen in Haiti that ran efficiently. All his equipment was placed on a long table. To the right were two basins, one filled with alcohol and the other with water for the sterilization and cleaning of his instruments. To the left were thick-handled pliers with fearsome jaws of assorted sizes, shapes and angles, each designed for specific teeth, whether upper or lower, incisors or molars. These redoubtable implements are rarely seen in the offices of American dentists, since they are used to extract teeth rather than repair them. In the middle was Jerry's daughter, a teenager with a rare look of innocence, preparing syringes with long thin needles for administering Novocaine. Two chairs were in front of the table where one patient would have his teeth pulled while the other waited for the Novocaine to take effect.

Jerry had good common sense and did not export the technology of his thriving orthodontic practice. No attempt was made to repair cavities or put on braces. The patient sat down, pointed to a tooth and if Jerry felt extraction was warranted, out it came. He did not have a paucity of patients. To the Haitians, Jerry represented a way of ridding themselves of chronic intractable pain. As I watched his forearm muscles bulge, I realized that brute strength along with finesse was needed.

After watching Jerry pull out several teeth, I was ready. My first patient, a brave unknowing young man, sat down and pointed to a rotting upper incisor. Slowly, I impaled the gum in front of the tooth with a long dental needle, giving a liberal dose of Novocaine. Next I anesthetized behind the palate, doing this more quickly, as it is painful. My patient did not even wince. Grabbing a mammoth pair of dental pliers, I grasped the tooth below the gum line and rocked it, feeling the laxity increase with each movement. Finally, I yanked down hard and out it came. The root that had been submerged under the gum was the same size as the visible tooth. Proud of my new skill, I pulled out several more incisors, using only male patients, since they did not shriek.

Feeling confident, I decided to pull out a molar. Molars, the crunching teeth in the back of the mouth, are more difficult to extract because of their awkward location. Also, unlike the solitary root of incisors, molars have three roots anchoring them to the jaw bone. I gave the patient twice the usual dose of Novocaine and grasped the tooth with the pliers that had its jaws oriented at a right angle to the handle. Rocking the tooth more to the outside than the inside, Jerry said that this decreased the chance of breaking the roots, I gradually loosened the molar. I gave a quick tug but it would not budge outward. After one minute of this wrestling, I could see my patient becoming uncomfortable, the clue being tears streaming down his otherwise stoic face. Putting his well-being in front of my ego, I asked Jerry for help. Within one second of his grasping the pliers, the tooth was out. He consoled me by saying all the work had already been done.

Any child who had a tooth pulled received a free toothbrush with toothpaste. Predictably, the adults said they wanted one, too. They even encouraged their children to have normal teeth pulled to obtain one. We had to stop distributing them entirely. Imagine, having a normal tooth pulled just to get a toothbrush to sell for one gourde, twenty American cents.

Since the demand was so great, I sometimes had to pull teeth without the help of a dentist. One young man came to me with a toothache. I examined him, found a rotten molar and told him he needed it to be extracted.

"But my wife is pregnant," he responded.

I had only been in Haiti several months and, thinking I did not understand him, asked him to repeat himself.

I had understood him correctly but, bewildered, I still made him repeat his statement slowly until it finally dawned on me that I was dealing with a superstition. I told him that taking out his tooth would not harm his unborn child. He politely acknowledged my viewpoint; however, he refused to allow me to extract his tooth. The Haitians had many superstitions but most were more pragmatic than this gentleman. Perhaps the pain was not yet severe enough.

Every time I worked in the clinics, I would see a patient that belonged in a medical textbook. In medical school, this is called a "classic" presentation. It is the way a sick patient is supposed to look.

For example, a man having a heart attack should be an overweight, over-worked 60-year-old – his clenched fist on his chest and sweat dripping from his brow – who says that after eating a large meal, he walked briskly up a flight of stairs in cold weather and suddenly experienced a dull ache that in the left side of his chest that rapidly crescendoed to a crushing pain that spread to his shoulder and left arm. In the real world, heart attack patients do not read the textbooks. Some complain of mild indigestion; others just have jaw pain. Some do not have any symptoms at all. They simply arrive for their checkup one day and their doctor sees the heart attack on a routine electrocardiogram (EKG), a test that analyses the forces of the heart muscle. In actuality, classic presentations are the exception, not the norm. However, they are more frequent in populations that either ignore or do not have access to medical care.

One woman gave a complaint to a visiting doctor. He did not know Creole, but when he examined her he noted a rapidly pounding pulse and asked me to look at her. As I watched her walk over to me, I could see tuberculosis written all over her. Gaunt and weak, she needed help sitting on the wooden chair beside me. When she took her shirt off, I could see her heart beating through her thin chest. Her pulse was 130. The normal pulse in healthy adults is near 70 but in my clientele, the anemic and malnourished Haitians, it was closer to 100. I listened to her heart. The sounds were loud but she had no murmur.

I also listened to her lungs, expecting to hear the wheezes of tuberculosis, but they were completely clear.

Like a typical American physician I immediately considered cancer as a possibility, but further examination revealed the classic signs of another problem. When I tapped her kneecap with my reflex hammer, her calf flew up into the air, amusing the other patients who kept asking me to do it again. Her blood pressure was 150/60, high for a young woman. There were random contractions of small muscle groups on her legs, fasiculations, which looked like areas of bobbing gelatin. The key sign was in front of her neck, where a mass bulged beside her windpipe. When I put my stethoscope on it, I could hear blood rushing through it. It was her overactive thyroid gland.

I had seen cases of hyperthyroidism before – it is fairly common – but never to this extreme. Usually only one or two signs are present when the disease is diagnosed. It is rare to see an American patient with a bulging thyroid, rapid pulse, brisk reflexes, high blood pressure, and fasiculations all at the same time. Every physician knows hyperthyroidism is common, so the threshold for screening for it is low. Most hospitals even do thyroid testing as part of their routine blood work, so it is detected before the patient is symptomatic.

The definitive treatment is to either surgically remove the thyroid or destroy it with radioactive iodine. With my facilities, these were not viable options, so I treated her medically with a drug called Inderal. It did not eliminate her hyperthyroidism, but at least some of her symptoms abated so she was comfortable.

Haiti is ideal for the connoisseur of venereal disease. My typical clinic was replete with eroded penises, abscessed vaginas, and huge groin lymph nodes from syphilis, gonorrhea, and chlamydia. Even in the industrialized world, patients will ignore horrible genital lesions because they are embarrassed, or delude themselves into thinking they will disappear.

Syphilis especially ravaged the Haitians because, when untreated, it could spread anywhere in the body. Only recently controlled in the United States, syphilis infected 5% of the American population at the turn of the century. It decreased because gonorrhea, which became an epidemic in the 1960's, has a shorter incubation period but is treated with the same drug, Penicillin. Consequently, subclinical syphilis is eradicated when gonorrhea is treated.

Although syphilis is considered to be a disease of the poor, it is not uncommon for a respected God-fearing member of the community to be hospitalized for a symptom that proves to be reactivated syphilis. For the sake of the patient's reputation and domestic tranquility, the diplomatic physician treats the disease without telling the family or documenting it.

Syphilis has a fascinating history. Its existence in pre-Columbian North America has been proven by the syphilitic bones found in Indian gravesites. Columbus' sailors probably carried it to Europe where it rapidly spread across the Continent. Called the "Great Pox" because of its characteristic rash, it made its way into Elizabethan literature. In France having a syphilitic rash was fashionable among the sexually avant-garde aristocracy.

Many Haitians come to the clinic with the first stage of syphilis, a painless ulcer – or chancre – on the genitalia. The chancre regresses whether treated or not. The difference is that with the Penicillin the syphilis is eradicated, whereas without it the infection silently percolates, eventually causing rash, fever, and swollen lymph nodes – the second stage. When treated at this stage, syphilis can still be cured without complications.

The real horror of syphilis is when it progresses to the tertiary stage, where its effects are devastating. It can attack the skin and eat through, destroying everything in its path. One of my patients had a huge abyss between her left eye and upper jaw that extended to the middle of her face, eradicating her nose. I could peer into this crater and see her teeth growing through her upper jaw in front of her palate.

The heart, brain, and spinal cord were also fair game. Tertiary syphilis attacks the aorta, rendering its valve incompetent and causing intractable heart failure. It destroys the part of the spinal cord that allows one to perceive pain. These patients would get ulcers on the bottom of their feet and never know it. When infected the disease would painlessly spread to the ankle joint, resulting in a crippled and unemployable patient sentenced to a life of begging. Other patients had deteriorating mental functions, becoming forgetful, irrational, and belligerent. Many Haitians have no concept of mental illness and would abuse or ostracize those afflicted, thinking they were possessed by the devil.

I quickly learned that any complaint from a fever, to an inflamed eye, to a foot ulcer could be masquerading as syphilis and warranted an examination of the genitalia along with at least a query about previous lesions.

Other venereal diseases also progressed to horrendous states. One type spread from the genitalia to groin lymph nodes that then ruptured through the skin. Unlike syphilis, these pus-draining abscesses required a month of oral antibiotics – Tetracycline four times a day.

Only the most compulsive patients will obediently take a pill four times a day, and few Haitians fell into this category. Furthermore, Tetracycline is considered to be a panacea and is hawked by street vendors to cure anything from diarrhea to ingrown toenails. My patients would sell it, especially when they were hungry. When it comes to food versus medicine – food always wins.

When I noticed my patients were not improving, I gently urged them with my tactful American bedside manner to take the medicine. This approach failed miserably. I soon realized that subtle suggestions were a waste of time. With no attempt at diplomacy, I told my patients to take the medicine or forget sex. This they feared more than any Voodoo god. My cure rate increased dramatically.

After seeing thousands of sick Haitians, I learned how to treat their problems. Nonetheless, I was occasionally reminded of American medicine. One elderly man came to the clinic complaining of difficulty in breathing. He managed a weak smile with his blue lips even though he was inspiring deeply at a high rate. His legs were swollen and he had a scrotum the size of a grapefruit. When I auscultated his barrel shaped chest, I could barely hear the air struggling to move through his damaged lungs. He had emphysema. It was so bad that his heart was weakened from constantly trying to push fluid through the non-compliant lungs. Consequently, the fluid trying to enter the heart backed up, causing the swelling.

A common problem in the United States, emphysema is rare in Haiti because the poor cannot afford its most common cause – cigarettes. This man managed, though, and not realizing the connection to his present state, proudly told me he had smoked a pack a day since he was eight. Emphysema accompanied by heart failure carries a poor prognosis anywhere. In a sense, he was lucky. In the United States, he would have spent his last year in a living hell – frequenting hospitals to have a tube rammed down his throat so that he could be placed on a respirator. Here, I just put him in Sans Fil and allowed him to die quickly and peacefully.

Unfortunately, there will soon be more patients like this in the Third World. Cigarette companies, with their shrinking markets in the industrial world, are pushing their product aggressively on developing nations. Smoking cigarettes in Haiti is synonymous with increasing status. Every up-and-coming Haitian male smokes.

Working in the clinics is where I learned the most. The Haitians taught me about tropical medicine and about themselves. It was wonderful to be a physician and only worry about your patients. I was free from the drudgery of endless paperwork and meaningless ritual. I was not forced by legal considerations to inconvenience my patients with silly tests to confirm the obvious or rule out the ridiculous. My patients trusted me and thanked me, even when I could do little to help.

There was a dark side, though. The volume was so overwhelming that I could not help everyone. The mothers stood there with their pleading eyes asking me to save their dying children. It simply could not be done. I had to choose who would live and who would die. I sometimes got depressed, but I made the decisions. Someone had to. But I never got used to it, and I knew that no matter how long I stayed in Haiti – I never would.

Chapter 3

The Home For the Dying

Lavi sa-a, se boukante mizè pou traka.
In this life, one trades misery for trouble.

Haitian proverb

Sans Fil was a most depressing place. It was here that the best the human race had to offer, the sisters , cared for the products of the worse conditions the human race could produce, the patients. They found them lying in gutters, crawling in garbage dumps, thrown into the Depot or dropped off at the front door. They were the handicapped, the elderly, the retarded and the abused. They were prostitutes with AIDS, men beaten by the Tonton Macoutes, and disease-infested skeletons breathing their last breaths. The sisters did not delude themselves into thinking they could help everyone at Sans Fil and had appropriately named it "The Home for the Dying." They saw these patients no differently from the way in which personnel in the growing Hospice movement view those with metastatic cancer or progressive senility. They were to be kept comfortable and loved and die with a smile on their face.

Nonetheless, the sisters wanted to cure those with treatable diseases. They distributed medicine, gave intravenous solutions and kept records. Unlike most missions in Haiti, the Missionaries of Charity had plenty of equipment. Generous donors sent everything—intravenous solutions, bandages, sutures, vitamins, medicines—crates upon crates of them. Frequently, I had to take time away from patient care to help the sisters figure out what to do with this plethora of equipment. Even the Haitian government did not dare block the flow of medical supplies to Mother Teresa's order.

I was helped at Sans Fil by Day and Nick. Day had just graduated from Brown University and opted to spend a year in Haiti before entering medical school. A muscular former college wrestler, he had short blond hair, blue eyes, a square jaw and a bull neck. Even this environment could not hide his preppiness. When he wore his green boxer shorts, he grabbed the matching green stethoscope. I always teased him; I told him he should be doing milk commercials or posing for corn flakes boxes. Nick was a college student from England and a dead ringer for Errol Flynn. Good-natured and gregarious, he was unsure of his future plans but was considering joining the priesthood.

I had given them a crash course on how to be a doctor; I taught them the physical exam, treatment of common diseases and basic procedures. They did spinal taps and thorocenteses, draining fluid from the chest, which are procedures performed only by physicians in the United States. They instinctively grasped everything I showed them, but more important, they cared. They cared enough to learn Creole in a matter of weeks, something American foreign affairs personnel rarely bothered to do. I constantly relied on their judgment.

I made rounds at Sans Fil in the early afternoon, when the temperature topped one hundred degrees. Irate after just escaping death at the hands of the Tap-Tap drivers on Rue Delmas, I would be tempted to forego rounds until I saw my favorite patient, Cosa Mala. Cosa guarded Sans Fil.

Daily I asked him, "Sak pase?", "What's happening?"

"Cosa Mala," he responded with a distant look of terror.

Thus he was named "Cosa Mala"—Spanish for "bad thing."

Many Haitians speak Spanish because they have worked in the Dominican Republic cutting sugar cane or constructing roads, low-paying back-breaking work that the Dominicans refuse to do even though their unemployment rate is 30%. Cosa Mala did little more than exist. Crippled from the contractions of his leg flexors, he could only propel himself by a crab-like walk. His thick wide forehead protruded over his vacuous eyes. As he rambled incoherently, his broad nose flared and his open mouth revealed fiery inflamed gums that suspended his black, cavity-infested teeth. Occasionally he sat on a chair but he preferred the concrete floor. His drooling saliva attracted flies he had no interest in dispersing. The other patients treated him as a pet rather than a human being and I am embarrassed to admit that I found myself doing the same.

I never figured out what was wrong with Cosa Mala, but my instincts told me he was once a normal, functioning human being who had suffered a tragedy. Perhaps the scars on his head were the result of a beating that left him permanently brain-damaged. Maybe he had suffered from brain-damaging meningitis, then again, it was possible he was simply psychotic.

When I walked over to him, he would stare at me and plead, "Anmwe! Anmwe!", "Help! Help!"

Cosa Mala's needs were very basic. He wanted either food or a cigarette. He could devour a huge bowl of rice in minutes, licking the bowl completely clear. I always gave him a cigarette, seeing little sense in denying him his greatest pleasure in order to prevent diseases he would not live long enough to develop. He would inhale deeply, holding the nicotine and charcoal in his lungs as long as possible, savoring the taste before expertly ejecting the smoke out through his nostrils. His enjoyment was sensual, and would have been a persuasive advertisement for cigarettes.

Attempts to cure or rehabilitate Cosa Mala were fruitless. One red-hot internist fresh from his residency at the Mayo Clinic treated him for the entire gamut of reversible dementias with Penicillin, Vitamin B-12, thiamine and other assorted concoctions. Others tried to teach him to walk, stretching his fused tendons until tears came to his eyes. I did not discourage these efforts, since I had made similar futile attempts.

But everyday when I asked, "Sak pase?"

He responded "Cosa Mala," with a distant look of terror.

Cosa Mala was an example of someone who simply needed a place to live – a permanent fixture at Sans Fil. As time passed, I learned those patients I could help and those I could not. However, acquiring this judgment was the most emotionally draining experience I had in Haiti. As any other physician would do, I began by erring on the side of over treatment. In doing so, I became depressed as I realized my limitations. Many patients were going to die regardless of my diagnostic acumen and intervention.

One of the first to teach me this hard reality was Theresa Louis. She was a bedridden twenty-year old woman who had diarrhea. She desperately clutched at my arm and implored me to save her. Yet she had the look of someone who was dying and knew it, a look every physician learns within weeks of beginning internship. Her mouth was parched, her eyeballs sunken and her systolic blood pressure 60. She was severely dehydrated, so I placed a large bore intravenous needle in her arm and within an hour had given her a liter of fluid. Her blood pressure increased to 80, but she appeared the same. I figured that when her diarrhea stopped, she would improve.

It never stopped. I tried everything. I pored over her stool specimen with my microscope, observing the multitude of worms and protozoa that flourished in her intestine. I read and reread my tropical medicine textbooks, weeding through the verbiage for the single sentence that would save her. I never found it. Her case became my obsession. I tried antibiotics, anti-parasitics, anti-malarials, vitamins and anti-tuberculosis medicines. The diarrhea still flowed. Thinking her problem may be polypharmacy—too many medicines—I stopped everything. The diarrhea still flowed.

"Doktè Joe, ban m' lavi," "Doctor Joe, give me life," she pleaded.

But she slowly worsened. Here was a woman younger than I, dying. Soon she refused intravenous fluid, wisely observing that it increased her diarrhea and made her body swell. If she lay on her left side, only that side swelled, giving her a macabre appearance.

I did not know what to do and there was no one to ask. She could not absorb any food because she was too malnourished to regenerate the villi in her intestine. She was malnourished because she could not absorb food. One day she gave up, refusing to eat or take medicine. At this point, I gave up, too. Eventually she succumbed, unaware that her agony had contributed to my medical education.

Soon, I learned how to triage. In the first group were those like Cosa Mala, who just needed a place to stay. Like the grandparents deposited in the hospital where I interned so that their families could vacation, this group needed no medical care, only food and human contact. As a matter of fact, treating these people made them worse.

The second group was those who were dying. As my experience increased, so did the number of patients in this category. Initially, my assessment was based on concrete data— blood pressure, heart rate, muscle mass and respiratory patterns. The sisters had a more accurate way of predicting death—by counting the number of flies hovering above the patient. As the patients faded the flies came, swarming over their faces, and feasting on their excrement. Those who were strong enough covered themselves with sheets but the severely debilitated had to tolerate them.

Evelyn was such a patient. She was an elderly woman who just wanted to die in peace. When I saw her, she was lying under a blanket with her hands, white from anemia, covering her face to protect her from the flies.

She was ancient, at least 80-years-old. Her wrinkled forehead gave way to thin dark eyebrows underneath which her eyes—the pupils opaque from cataracts—attempted to discern me. She was toothless, and her lips rolled inside her mouth so that the vermillion border was invisible. The other women braided her short gray hair so that she had the appearance of a horned owl.

Her face did not look as if it possessed the wisdom of the ages, only a semi-content look of satisfaction. She was a survivor. She had survived numerous childbirths, batterings from sexually-aggressive belligerent men, the American occupation, Papa Doc and the Tonton Macoutes. But she was resigned to accepting her destiny.

I gently lifted the blanket in order to examine her. Around her neck were rosary beads, arcing over her collar bone and tracing the contours of the crevices between her prominent ribs. The flesh on her back was sculptured by her vertebrae and the scapulae—two triangles below her shoulders. Her taut skin stretched over her pelvis, showing the architecture of this complex bone as it curved to form the pubis under which all her children had passed. She had probably outlived them all. Her legs were spindles. Unable to verbalize her objection to my rude interruption, she defecated, unabashed by her state, not wanting to be cleaned, only to be left alone, to die and meet whatever deity she believed in.

After seeing patients like Evelyn day in and day out, I began to wonder what I was doing in Haiti. It was beyond my comprehension that people could be subject to such misery. What had they done to deserve this? I could see no value in their suffering. Many were so young, younger than I – yet I could not save them.

Slowly, I began to accept my limitations. With dying patients, my job was to comfort, not cure. Historically, this has been the role of the physician. It is only recently that effective treatments have been found for heart failure, asthma, syphilis and tuberculosis. The potions used to treat these diseases at the turn of the century were useless and often dangerous as well.

With the sisters' help, I mastered the art of caring for the dying so that patients like Evelyn could die with dignity, with a smile on their face. The sisters kept the dying clean and fed those who had the energy to swallow. I did my best to see they were comfortable.

One of my first actions was to cover the dying patients with mosquito nets. The problem was that Sans Fil had no air conditioning and some patients preferred the persistent flies to the choking heat under the nets. Flies did not cause the visceral revulsion in Haitians that they did in me. At times, I thought I was just treating myself. Also the Haitians, perceptive people, realized that when I covered someone with a net, I expected that patient to die.

One even yelled at me, "M' p' ap mouri", "I'm not dying."

She was wrong.

Although empathy and compassion were important, they were not always enough. No amount of hand-holding and tender loving care could comfort patients who were in their early twenties and dying. They were being cheated and they knew it. These patients and those with intractable pain needed something more. With liberal doses of Valium and Demoral, I was able to comfort them. I would add these drugs to the intravenous solutions so that they received a constant infusion, since neither the sisters nor I had the time to constantly administer them. We had the eternal gratitude of these patients.

Even an intravenous solution by itself can be comforting. Dying patients do not have the energy to drink and become dehydrated, an unpleasant state, as anyone who jogs or plays tennis can testify

I will never forget one patient who was brought to Sans Fil. About 50-years-old, he weighed 65 pounds; the retracting facial skin taut on his skull made his beard look even more straggly. It did not take an infinite amount of wizardry to see that he was dying. Since he was severely dehydrated, I immediately placed an intravenous line. Even though I have started thousands of intravenous lines, it took me several attempts because his veins perforated so easily. When I was done, I stood up beside his bed.

He did not even look at me, but sensing that I had finished the procedure, he reflexively said in perfect unaccented English, "Thank you. Have a nice vacation."

Later that day, he died.

My third triage group was the treatable. These were the ones with which I spent most of my time. Here is where I could make a difference, by catching a reversible problem before it progressed.

One woman was brought to Sans Fil after she was found lying on the street of one of the slums. The Belgian priest who brought her told me that her husband got tired of listening to her whining and heaved her out of their house.

Theresa Pierre was exhausted and weak. Dressed in a tattered blue dress with a red bandanna tied around her head, she was a handsome woman of twenty with high cheekbones, robust lips and piercing black eyes. She did not appear malnourished. One thing I learned in Haiti is that a well-nourished patient who is acutely ill is often someone I can cure.

I extracted from her that she had "maltèt e lafyèv," "headache and fever." In Haiti, this is malaria until proven otherwise. However, upon examining her, I found her neck was so stiff that when I tried to lift her head, it elevated her upper body. She refused to bend her neck. In medical parlance, this is called "nuchal rigidity" and is seen in meningitis, an infection of the the lining that encases the brain, spinal cord and spinal fluid. Without treatment it can be fatal, and those who survive may have neurological damage such as paralysis, deafness, or impaired mental capacity.

The diagnosis is easily made by doing a spinal tap. Since this lining space, the meninges, extends past the termination of the spinal cord, one can take out spinal fluid by inserting a hollow needle with a stylet in between the vertebrae in the lower back. To the uninitiated, it is a terrifying procedure. The patient must curl up in a fetal position while a five inch needle penetrates the back. With proper anesthesia, there is little pain, but the idea of a needle impaling one's back is emotionally disconcerting.

Theresa Pierre voiced no objections as I positioned her. Being trained to always explain procedures to my patients, I informed her in simple Creole what I was about to do. She was so lethargic that she did not even cry or move as I plunged the large needle four inches into her back. Feeling the characteristic pop as I entered the meningeal sheath, I pulled out the stylet. Several drops of cloudy fluid dripped out. Spinal fluid should be clear.

Quite excited, I examined the fluid under my microscope. There were numerous white blood cells along with rare Gram negative rods, clinching the diagnosis. After searching through several boxes in our hopelessly unorganized dispensary, I found the same antibiotics I would have used in the United States, Ampicillin and Chloramphenicol. Of course they were expired, but beggars can not be choosers. The medicine must be given in a vein, so I put an intravenous line and gave the first dose myself.

Two days later, she did not seem much better as she lay there burning with fever, barely responsive. She had one good sign, however. When I restarted the intravenous line, she quickly arose from her somnolence, screeching "Ooyyee." Nonetheless, I wondered if she was receiving the proper antibiotics. I never knew what type of bacteria was causing the infection. In the United States, the laboratory would not only identify it, but also tell whether it was sensitive to the antibiotics being used. Here I just guessed and prayed.

The most difficult part about her care was keeping the intravenous line in her arm. Every day when I arrived it was out. The sisters were busy enough as it was. They could not do everything. So daily, against her objections, I restarted it and gradually she improved. After a week the fevers stopped and, figuring I could cut corners, I switched her to oral antibiotics. Meningitis should be treated with intravenous antibiotics for at least ten days. But this was Haiti. There was no attending or chief resident to tell me I was not following the accepted protocol.

It was a mistake. The next day, she spiked a fever. Cursing my stupidity, I restarted the intravenous line. Fortunately, the gods were kind and forgave me. She again improved, developing the key sign, an appetite. She never understood why she needed the intravenous line, screaming every time I placed it as if I were some sort of torturer. I tried to explain to her many times why she needed it, but she did not understand. She was an illiterate, superstitious peasant who had barely been conscious when she arrived. Now she was slowly improving, but was being told by this crazy blan who spoke the strangest Creole that she needed a needle in her arm. It made no sense to her. But I was not going to make the same mistake twice. Like it or not, she got the intravenous medicine every day until I was satisfied that the meningitis was eradicated.

One day I walked into the women's ward and she was standing there washing dishes. Since she was better, the sisters put her to work. She gave me a huge smile saying "Bon swa", "Good afternoon," realizing that all of my torture had cured her. Eventually she departed, healthy, thanking me profusely. The Haitians are very appreciative people, even if they are not sure about what you are doing.

Another reversible problem I treated was heart failure. Joseph, a young man brought from the Depot, suffered from shortness of breath. In the United States, this is either asthma or pneumonia. But when I listened to Joseph's lungs, it was obvious he had neither. I heard extra sounds called "rales," caused by extra fluid that has collected in the lung spaces. When the left side of the heart pumps poorly, the fluid backs up in the lungs and the patient can not breathe. In older patients, heart failure usually occurs because a previous heart attack has weakened the muscle or high blood pressure is making the heart work too hard. In young patients, it is congenital, caused by either a malfunctioning valve or a hole in the wall between the chambers.

In the Third World, there is another cause – thiamine deficiency. Thiamine, one of the B vitamins, is ubiquitous in nature, but there is not much in sugar cane – which is all poor Joseph sucked on. Without thiamine, the heart muscle contracts inefficiently.

Joseph, good-natured and optimistic, did well. I gave him a mild diuretic, allowing him to slowly lose the excess fluid. Meanwhile, I gave him megadoses of intravenous thiamine. It took time – almost a month – but eventually Joseph was breathing comfortably.

Many patients at Sans Fil came from the Depot, a walled-off area beside the Hôpital Général. Here the rejects from the hospital were strewn on the ground – dying, insolvent, and too weak to move. In spite of the conditions, there is a communal atmosphere. Those able to walk care for those who can not.

Menm nan lanfè gen moun pa.
Even in hell there is friendship.

Along the walls are stacks of cardboard which are spread out at night to sleep on. Food, usually a small bowl of rice, is distributed twice a day. Unlike the rest of Haiti, no one here asked me for anything. They knew their situation was hopeless. They were beyond begging.

Actually, the Depot's condition has improved since the sisters received the government's permission to make it habitable. The piles of garbage that attracted monstrous rats have been removed. Those brought to Sans Fil no longer have gnawed holes on their faces. The new drainage system presents flooding during tropical deluges, so that those too feeble to move no longer drown.

During my stay in Haiti, I came to know the Depot well. Everyone there came to know me, too. Many patients I had cured would arrive there three months later with another problem, usually stemming from malnutrition or homelessness.

The first Depot patient I encountered was a young man lying on the ground. The Tonton Macoutes had beaten him with their favorite weapon, a club with a protruding nail. His crime was organizing a borlette or lottery—Haiti's national pastime. The Haitians, like most poor, are fanatical gamblers. As the proverb goes:

> Si ou pa jwe, ou pa ka genyen.
> If you don't play, you can't win.

They put their fate in the hands of their gods. I suspect his real crime, though, was not making large enough pay-offs to the Tonton's. Well-nourished and muscular, he was not a typical Depot patient. Until the gods had frowned on him, he had been prospering by Haitian standards. Between the sinews of his thigh, a large abscess had formed around one of the puncture wounds; its pain had made him an invalid. He greeted me with a warm smile. He knew I was there to help. There was no fever, but the lymph nodes in his groin above the abscess were swollen. Lymph nodes are glands that fight an infection in an area they drain. This is the reason they may swell up in the neck during a sore throat or cold.

The sisters took him to Sans Fil. There, after giving him a local anesthetic, I made a large cut with a scalpel into the abscess and drained all the pus. We gave him Penicillin injections, and soon he was walking without pain. After several weeks, he departed a wiser man, more willing to allow the tonton's to extort from him. Depot patients could be helped if someone only took the time.

Gratifying as it was to cure people, I was just scratching the surface. Making someone healthy was easy when compared to making survival possible in a brutal country like Haiti. Sans Fil was a reprieve from reality, a chance to regain health before facing a hostile world. Many of our patients simply could not make it.

Louis was a classic example. He arrived at Sans Fil gaunt, febrile and coughing from tuberculosis. Two months later, the tuberculosis was under control. He had gained thirty pounds and was confident that he could now make a living. There was a problem; however, he had no place to go. Undaunted and sporting a huge smile, he left anyway, thanking all of us for helping him. His only possessions were a snapshot of himself taken by a generous visitor, a Liberty Bowl T-shirt, trousers, and a Minnesota Twins baseball cap. Two days later he was back. Day found him lying at the front door, tears streaming down his face, clutching his now tattered picture.

Day was prepared for anything; he was used to Haiti. Louis's shirt was filthy, the trousers torn and the cap, long gone. His eyes were sunken deep into his head and he had lost at least five pounds. He could barely responded to my questions.

"Do you have a family?"

"No."

"Friends?"

"No."

"Did you have a place to sleep?"

"No."

"Where did you sleep?"

"Under the tables in the market place with the crazy people."

"Did you eat anything?"

"No."

"Did you drink anything?"

"No."

There was no way he could survive in the real world of Haiti. This is why so many roamed the streets begging, looking for cars to clean, trying to do odd errands, or becoming prostitutes; it was that or nothing. Many Haitians could not get enough money together to buy food or rent a place to sleep. They forever roamed around, until some social organization helped them or, more commonly and tragically, they lay down and died.

Day made Louis some Kool-Aid. He did not have the strength to sit up, so I helped him. Now the tears really began to roll down his cheeks. As he gulped down the Kool-Aid, he said nothing; not even "mèsi." He was embarrassed and depressed. His pride was shattered and his self-esteem non-existent. He did not like being dependent on us. He returned when he felt the only alternative was death.

Medically, he was fine, but now he had a greater problem. Uneducated, illiterate, with no marketable skills, he had no earning power. To help him would require a huge investment. Someone had to pay his room and board while he learned a trade. There were hundreds of thousands like him. As I watched him weep, I realized how little I could change. I could cure tuberculosis, malaria and dysentery but I could not cure the disease of living in Haiti.

This scenario was repeated ad nauseam. The same thing happened to the women, the only difference being that upon returning, they were also pregnant.

Though I was discouraged, I felt I was acquiring the skills to render good medical care. However, the minute I got cocky was the minute I got burned.

A teenage girl, Caroline, complained that her legs hurt, especially when walking. With her high cheekbones, neatly braided hair and impeccable posture, she appeared healthy, with only a tinge of anemia in her skin. I examined her carefully, checking her muscular legs for atrophy and tenderness. Using my knuckles – I no longer carried a hammer – I checked her reflexes. Everything was normal. Her hips functioned, since I could elevate each leg until it formed a ninety-degree angle with her torso. She could bend her knees and rotate her ankles. Yet, she persisted with her complaint.

I had her walk, watching her grimace with each awkward step. She was either in considerable pain or a good actress. Compulsively repeating my examination, I again found nothing until I touched her right knee. It felt hot. How did I miss this the first time?

Sensing pay dirt, I pushed on her patella – the kneecap. Rather than meet resistance as it opposed the knee bones, it bobbed – ballotted – in a sea of fluid, fluid that should not be there.

Humbled once again, I grabbed a syringe to extract the fluid. I explained the problem to her. Rather than dismay, her cherubic smile indicated relief that I finally believed her. I stuck the needle in between the patella and knee bones, withdrawing clear yellow fluid.

Joint fluid aids in determining the cause of a swollen joint. An infected joint has cloudy white fluid, with many white blood cells and bacteria. In gout, one may see crystals. By putting a drop of fluid between the thumb and forefinger and rapidly separating them, one can get a crude idea of its viscosity. Non-infected fluid is viscous so that a string is formed. The "string test" is now regarded as hopelessly misleading, which it is, but in Haiti I needed all the help I could get.

Caroline's joint fluid formed a five inch string. Under the microscope, there were no crystals or bacteria, only a few white blood cells. She had a non-infected joint.

I asked her more questions and examined her for the third time. She did not fall on her knee, but volunteered that her hands were stiff, especially upon waking up. She also had fluid in her left elbow. Even with this crude assessment, I had enough information to diagnose rheumatoid arthritis. She had the juvenile variety, which is common but does not receive much publicity. Patting myself on the back, I came up with a brilliant treatment, aspirin and time.

In spite of its simplicity, the treatment worked, and Caroline was soon walking normally. It did not stop her from complaining; however, some of her complaints – such as worms crawling out of her mouth – were legitimate. She had reminded me that medicine is a humbling profession. There are no professors, just students at different stages of advancement.

The Haitians also taught me some of their medical treatments that were often more effective than mine. One time, I witnessed a woman go into intense mourning after her child succumbed – writhing on the floor, contorting her face, thrashing, kicking and screeching. The sisters looked at me, waiting for me to do something. I drew up a syringe of Valium and prepared to inject her, but she was moving so much that I was afraid a blind stab would injure her. I had no choice but to stand by and prevent her from hurting herself. Fortunately a Haitian woman came to my assistance. She lit a match, blew it out, and then applied the ashes to the mourning woman's scalp. Then she tied a half-square knot with the woman's hair over the ashes. The writhing stopped and this previously wild woman stood up and walked away, as if nothing had happened.

Several months later in the woman's ward, I was again faced with a patient reenacting the same scenario which the Haitians, incidently, called a "kriz." Not being an American medicine chauvinist, I lit a match, extinguished it, rubbed it on the woman's scalp and tied her hair over the ashes. Her "kriz" desisted and I proudly went on to my next patient while registering a new treatment in my armamentarium.

Although Haiti is replete with malnutrition, tuberculosis and dysentery, it also harbors bizarre tropical diseases. The sisters brought one such case to Sans Fil. When I first saw him, he was sitting in a chair wearing one of the donated gowns. He was middle-aged, graying and balding, and did not appear to be in any distress.

"Ki pwoblèm ou?", "What is your problem?", I asked.

He did not reply verbally, but dramatically lifted his gown revealing, to my horror, a scrotum the size of a basketball, a huge sack stretched to a size beyond imagination. He could not walk without placing a towel beneath his scrotum and suspending the weight with his hands. One of the sisters put it best when she remarked that she did not understand why God created such a terrible disease, wondering how this kind of suffering could possibly help this man. I had seen pictures of the problem in textbooks and knew the diagnosis, since pictures like this are not easily forgotten.

It was filariasis, a parasitic disease that is spread by mosquito bites. Immature forms of the parasite, filariae, enter the blood stream, are carried throughout the body, and eventually lodge in a lymph node. Here the filariae mature and reproduce, destroying the node and causing the area it drains to swell. This poor man was unfortunate enough to have the lymph nodes that drained his scrotum destroyed.

It can affect other areas, too. One of my patients had his leg so swollen that the skin became redundant and folded over itself, making his leg look like that of an elephant, a condition appropriately named elephantiasis. Another patient had a clitoris the size of an orange.

I told this man I would try to help him.

He quickly responded. "Ou pa kap ede m', sèlman Bondye kap ede m' ","You can't help me, only God can help me."

He was right. Once the lymph nodes were damaged, nothing could be done; however, medicine could prevent the filariasis from progressing. The medicine also chased the filariae into the blood stream before killing them, providing a method for making a positive diagnosis via microscopic examination. Thus I could check any one for filariasis. Day and Nick knew enough to obtain a blood sample on any one who had unilateral leg swelling. If I saw the serpentine filariae winding amidst the blood cells, we would give medicine for several weeks, preventing our patients from developing serious physical handicaps.

Although this patient was skeptical about my ability to help him, he did allow me to take his picture. When I first arrived in Haiti, I took pictures of everyone – even people on the street. The Haitians did not appreciate this and after several months in the country, I realized how rude I was. I would not like it if someone driving a Jaguar and wearing a Bijan suit stopped and took pictures of me while I was working and minding my own business. Upon realizing this, I asked permission before taking pictures and then negotiated a fair price.

When I got to the point where I thought nothing would surprise me, I would see something more bizarre than ever before. Some Haitian nuns brought in a comatose man they had found lying in front of their convent. They carried him out of their car and placed him on the concrete floor in front of the men's ward.

Only his nose rose above the sea of flies that immediately alit upon his face. They filled his eye sockets, crawled in and out of his nostrils and were dispersed by the foaming saliva that bubbled from his lips with each labored breath. The saliva dribbled down his chin and neck reaching his heavily-stained T-shirt. Along its trail, the flies jockeyed for position. Although I was hardened, this sight tested my digestive system. I felt my avocado lunch shoot up my esophagus.

It did not prevent me from making the diagnosis. He had rabies. Virtually non-existent in the United States, rabies is uniformly fatal unless treated early. It progresses though several stages, the most notable being the rabid stage, characterized by paroxysms of violence. Eventually, the patient slips into a coma and succumbs. There was nothing to be done for this poor man and he soon died. His image popped into my mind every time dogs chased me while I was riding my moped through the streets.

Although I saw more exotic disease in Haiti than in the United States, my main job was still nuts-and-bolts medical problems. One of these was "ascites," a collection of fluid in the abdomen. At any given time, it affected half-a-dozen patients at Sans Fil.

A patient with massive ascites looks as if he is pregnant. The skin over the abdomen is stretched tautly from the pubic bone to the bottom of the rib cage, giving it an iridescent sheen. The fluid pressure causes the umbilicus, the navel, to pop up, making the abdomen appear as a gently rounded hill with an observatory on top. Mild ascites is harder to diagnosis because it looks just like a pot belly. Since this was not a possibility in Haiti, anyone who had a distended abdomen had ascites until proven otherwise. I could confirm it by performing one of the lost arts of physical diagnosis, percussion.

In percussion, one places a finger flat on the skin and taps it with the index finger of the opposite hand. By the sound this makes, one can ascertain the nature of what is under the skin. If it is air, one hears tympany, but if it is fluid, a dull thud emanates. By percussing across the abdomen with the patient supine, one can determine where the air meets the fluid by hearing the sound change. If the point changes when the patient lies on his side, it is called "shifting dullness," a good indicator of ascites. Since X-rays and ultrasound are much more accurate, percussion is rarely done properly in the United States.

The treatment of ascites is a mild diuretic and bed rest. The key is to remove the fluid slowly to avoid dehydration. A problem arises in a patient with massive ascites, since the fluid impinging on the diaphragm gives the lungs less room to expand, resulting in shortness of breath. In this case, the fluid must be removed directly by draining it from the abdomen.

It is a simple procedure. It can be done safely by using an angiocath, which is a needle with a surrounding plastic catheter. The angiocath is attached to a syringe and inserted into the abdomen above the pelvis on the left side, since the liver and spleen are not in this area. When the abdominal cavity is entered, a straw-colored fluid fills the syringe. Now the needle is withdrawn so only the plastic catheter remains, minimizing the risk of injury if the patient moves. Two quarts of fluid are removed, resulting in easier breathing and a smiling patient. Unfortunately, the fluid returns unless the liver recuperates, which is not often.

A gamut of diseases can cause liver failure and subsequent ascites, but by far the most common is alcoholism. Richard was such a patient. The good sisters found Richard lying along Rue St. Joseph, Haiti's answer to the Bowery. Wearing a soiled blue-and-white plaid shirt and shredded urine-soaked gray trousers, Richard played the part well. The week-old stubble, the randomly strewn hair, the shoeless swollen feet and pale nonchalant lips all contributed to the effect. He greeted me by vomiting up blood on the floor between us. When he was done, he gave me the same nonchalant look. Richard had been doing some serious drinking.

Alcoholism is rare among the Haitians, but then Richard was not a Haitian. He was a transplanted French-Canadian, the only white to ever come to Sans Fil. Thanks to the rude personal questions from visitors, Richard's story later unfolded. He had married a Haitian and was living happily ever after until she became disgusted with his drinking and physically escorted him from her premises. Since then, Richard had not fared well, subsisting until his money evaporated, at which point he ended up in the Hôpital Général. He claimed that the Haitian doctors treated him with a novel approach, bringing him various types of Barbancourt rum, and having him compare the one, three and five-star varieties.

It was a vast improvement over "clarin," the 20-cent-a-bottle rum made from fermented sugar cane roots that he had been drinking before his admission. When this method failed to cure him they discharged him, and after several days of aimless wandering he was found by the sisters.

"How much do you drink a day?", I asked.

"A bottle of clarin." At least he was honest.

"Do you have a problem with alcohol?"

"Not at all," but in the same breath he continued "I'll never touch the stuff again, never, never, never..."

There was no sense in asking any more questions. There had not even been any sense in asking the initial ones – so I examined him. His skin as well as the normally white eyes were yellow with jaundice. His liver was tender when I pressed over it, and his distended abdomen had shifting dullness. The blood he had vomited was from his bleeding stomach ulcer, and his right foot had a huge abscess on it.

Richard brought me back to my internship, the sleepless nights I had spent admitting drunks so they would not go home and use their hapless wives as punching bags. He upset me. Here in the midst of unspeakable squalor, this lowlife invaded. Everyone else at Sans Fil was a victim of circumstances beyond their control, but not Richard. He was a self-imposed loser.

In medical school, I was taught alcoholism is just another disease like pancreatitis or diabetes. It sounded sensible then, but now I no longer agreed. He had been born into a free industrialized country and not only ended up as an alcoholic, but as an alcoholic in Haiti. Nick and Day thought it was funny, but it did not amuse me. My feelings embarrassed me – this was not appropriate thinking for a physician – but I could not change the way I felt.

Unable to handle the situation, I dumped everything on Nick and Day. I had cared for this problem so many times that the treatment was forever inculcated in my mind – put in an intravenous line, give ampules of thiamine, folic acid and B12, put in a nasogastric tube and lavage the stomach, give an antacid, drain the abscess, etc. The ascites was not symptomatic, so it did not need to be drained. I wrote down everything that needed to be done and walked away.

Like most alcoholics, Richard was indestructible. He improved quickly. The jaundice cleared, the ulcer stopped bleeding, the ascites resorbed and the abscess healed. He rapidly gained weight and self-respect, showering, shaving and grooming his hair. He became a model patient, attending church and helping with the sicker patients. Then, as quickly as he came, he left. Several months later a friend of mine spotted him at Rue Ste. Joseph. I would not let him tell me about Richard. I did not want to know. I wanted to live a lie and pretend he had not started drinking again.

All the patients at Sans Fil received the best care possible. Even though many were sedentary, bedsores were infrequent, much rarer than in American nursing homes. It was because the sisters took the necessary care to prevent them. To them, nursing was a vocation, not just a job.

Nonetheless, working at Sans Fil was difficult. A government van arrived daily to pick up the dead. Uniformed men with their poker faces carted away the bodies, the skeletons of sagging flesh that had lost their humanity long before they had died. They were piled into the van, their eyes opened widely, staring at me. They were the victims of an economic concentration camp, killed by the slow but sure genocide of malnutrition and disease. As they gazed at me, there was a glimmer of recognition in their eyes: the doctor who placed an intravenous line so they would not die thirsty, the doctor who snowed them with morphine because no amount of tender loving care could comfort a dying man in his twenties.

The worst part about Sans Fil is that it represented Haiti perfectly. For every patient there, given a bed, food, medicine and a brief respite, there were hundreds gallantly struggling for a gourde so they could buy something to eat.

Even in death, the Haitians were exploited. The bodies could be reclaimed by their families but at a cost of thirty dollars, over a month's wages. The government workers knew the superstitious Haitian peasants would pay because of their Voodoo belief that the body had to be properly buried to prevent it from returning as a zombie.

Visitors frequently came to observe. They were a diverse crowd ranging from idealistic college students to religious zealots. There were Club Med stragglers who wanted to absorb the Haitian experience. They asked me about the incidence of venereal disease, especially AIDS, then returned to Club Med. There were American nuns with their stretch pants, Nike sneakers, Lacrosse shirts and Minolta cameras, wondering why I was not smart enough to figure out they were nuns. There were the sixties leftovers in their wide-wale corduroys and sleeveless T-shirts, with their bald heads, thick sideburns and bifocal wire-rimmed glasses. There were doctors vacationing from their suburban practices, making useless suggestions to which I responded with a polite smile.

None of them ever stayed long. As they watched Day, Nick, the sisters and me work, they commented how wonderful it was to see us helping the poorest of the poor. Deep down, I am sure they felt I was crazy. Perhaps they were right. A card I received from my Belgian doctor friend best summarized the situation. On the front was an elephant on a seesaw with a bunch of mice on the other end. The elephant was suspended in the air by the weight of the mice and had a disconcerted look on its face. He wrote my name on the elephant.

Chapter 4

The Children's Home

Tout maladi pa maladi doktè.
Not every disease can be cured by a doctor.

Haitian Proverb

While working the clinics saved the most lives, working in the Children's Home was the most fun. Nursing a sick child to health while watching the joy on the mother's face is the most gratifying experience in medicine.

The Children's Home housed 60 children whose ages ranged from 4 months to 12 years. Newborns were not admitted because of the myriads of diseases they could contract. Most were temporary residents to be returned to their families when they became healthy; others were orphans awaiting adoption. Some with chronic diseases had become permanent residents because they required constant care and attention.

Unlike Sans Fil, where the philosophy was to comfort the dying, the sisters tried to cure the patients in the Children's Home. Although the sisters did not receive formal medical training, they had learned clinical medicine from their extensive practical experience.

Two sisters slept at the Children's Home every night like permanent interns. As they were willing to do anything to keep a child alive, I had to be firm in my requests that they sleep or else they would labor all night.

The Children's Home was my first and last stop of the day. Leaving my apartment in central Port-au-Prince, I threaded my moped through the traffic on Avenue John Brown and Avenue Martin Luther King. As I arrived, shoeless, shirtless children chased me, asking for money or at least a ride. The sisters never ceased to amaze me with the misery they uncovered – an abandoned blind infant, a six-month-old that weighed seven pounds, or a child with his face swollen from malnutrition and renal failure.

The facility itself was an eminently practical white one-story building with four bedrooms, a playroom and a storage room. Over the entrance was a black baby doll with Caucasian features holding a sign that said "WELCOME." Upon entering, I would be inundated by a half-a-dozen smiling children with newly-acquired pot bellies and chubby cheeks chattering, "Doktè Joe, Doktè Joe," and begging to be picked up. This gave me tremendous satisfaction since I could remember them when they were more dead than alive.

Since malnutrition had stunted their growth, these children were much older than their size indicated. Most were delayed developmentally and learned to crawl, stand and walk later than American children. At first this confused me because a Haitian child the size of an American eight-month-old would be walking, a landmark that occurs at twelve to sixteen months. I had to learn to increase my age estimate until I became accustomed to the smaller Haitian children.

The largest bedroom had red and white walls covered with religious icons including a black Madonna and Child. There were twenty-five cribs, steel contraptions covered with lead-based white paint that the children sucked on, one of the many safety hazards. The healthy babies, in their cloth diapers and American T-shirts, were standing with a firm grasp on the railing, first pensively peering at me and then at the Haitian women distributing food. None were crying. They were just waiting patiently for their turn.

One poor child with opaque cataracts, either from rubella or syphilis, rolled his hands on his face and then banged his head against the side rails, a form of self-stimulation to compensate for his lack of vision. Even if the cataracts were removed, his vision would be poor because he was already too old to learn how to the interpret visual images transmitted from his eyes to his brain.

Another child, Stephan, has a nine-month-old body attached to a head the size of a volleyball. He has hydrocephalus, a condition caused by inadequate drainage of the spinal fluid in the skull. The pressure build-up causes the skull bones to separate, rather than fuse. A flashlight pressed against his head gave it an eerie red glow, a phenomenon known as "transillumination" in medical parlance. When he became dehydrated, his head shrunk like a deflated volleyball. We just kept him clean and comfortable, bandaging the skin ulcers on his head, making him a turbaned sultan who commanded the immediate attention of all the do-gooders who visited.

The mothers stayed with their children, cleaning and feeding them and sleeping under their cribs at night. Although concerned and dedicated, they lacked basic knowledge of mothering. For example, they did not know how to feed their children.

Like Italian grandmothers, they believed a stuffed baby was a happy baby. I became irate as I watched them shovel food into their children's mouths, invariably resulting in the child's vomiting or developing diarrhea. Children are smart. If a child refuses to eat, there is a reason. Either the child is full, or is too sick to have an appetite. In either case, pushing food down his throat only results in continual floor cleaning.

The Haitian women had the survival instinct, a need to stock up on food when available. I instructed them to feed their children slowly and not force food upon them. They would smile vacuously and nod politely, humoring me until I was out of sight, then continue to shovel food down their children's mouths.

Once a child improved, the mother would leave. The child was now being housed and fed free. The mothers knew the sisters regarded motherhood as sacred and would never allow a child to be adopted without the mother's consent. When she did eventually return, the sisters would make her take her child.

Some mothers realized they simply could not care for their children and would give them up for adoption. These children were sent to an industrialized country such as Belgium or Canada with a ticket to a fulfilling life. Rarely did they go to the United States because of the multiple demands required to get the paperwork through the bureaucracy. By the time the adoption was approved for the United States, the child would be eligible for a driver's license.

One night, as I was leaving for Pétionville to have an overpriced beer, I noticed a child crawling on the road. Picking him up, I brought him into the Children's Home. He was surprisingly healthy, only slightly malnourished. The next day the sisters called the police and a lawyer and officially adopted the child. This prevented anyone from claiming him. Within a month, he was in Switzerland, making some couple very happy.

In Haiti, poor children are sometimes raised by the wealthy in return for domestic service. Unfortunately, this is not the only service they are asked to provide. The girls are expected to furnish wealthy adolescents with hands-on sexual instruction. This ultimate in child abuse is not unique to Haiti and is routinely condemned by international human rights organizations. Nonetheless, it will continue to flourish as long as families can not afford to feed their children.

As at Sans Fil, I concentrated on the patients who had life-threatening illnesses. I personally examined these children daily, weighing them, taking their temperature, collecting blood, sputum and stool specimens, changing their medicine, starting intravenous lines and putting in nasogastric tubes. None of the children had just a simple problem, but a host of diseases such as malaria, typhoid fever and worms.

With little diagnostic equipment, my judgement was paramount. A gradual weight gain was a key sign. It meant the child was eating properly. A rapid increase indicated excess fluid accumulation from heart or renal failure, whereas weight loss signified a poor appetite.

However, the most important sign was a spontaneous smile, something a sick child rarely does. Haitian children do not cry unless there is a good reason, such as hunger, discomfort or lethargy. The Haitian women discourage such behavior with a swift slap to the side of the head. When I gave a child too much attention, the women would warn me that he would "vin gate", "become spoiled." They were right. Veterans of the Children's Home knew that a healthy howl commanded my immediate attention. Nonetheless, when a Haitian child cried and I could not find a reason, I would later discover I had missed a diagnosis.

The most common problem was dehydration from diarrhea, and we always had at least six intravenous lines running to treat it. These are the children that oral rehydration could not help, who were so dehydrated they could not make tears and so weak they could not swallow liquids.

Jacqueline was typical. At nine months of age she weighed a strapping eight pounds, well below the fifth percentile. Her only remaining fat was on her cheeks; otherwise she was a collection of connected sticks, struggling feebly to resist my examination. When her mouth opened, no sound emanated—she was too weak to cry. Her skin tented when I pinched it and when I put my finger in her mouth, it did not even become damp. Jacqueline was dying from severe dehydration and needed an intravenous line immediately.

Finding a small vein in her hand, I threaded a needle into it. Jacqueline was lucky; I hit it on the first try. Unlike oral rehydration, rehydrating intravenously is fraught with complications. Babies are smarter than doctors; they know when they are getting too much fluid or if it is the wrong concentration and stop drinking it. When it is pouring into their veins, though, they can not exercise this option.

With Jacqueline, I had to choose the solution and its rate of entry. There were a variety of solutions available, ranging from those that were just sugar and water to those that approximated the concentration of sodium and chloride in blood. The latter is called normal saline, and there are various intermediate concentrations such as quarter-normal, half-normal and three-quarters-normal saline.

Choosing the proper solution depends on the blood concentration of the sodium. For example, a child with a high sodium should have a dilute intravenous solution, such as quarter-normal saline. However, it must be given slowly to allow equilibration by the kidneys. Rapid changes can cause seizures and brain damage. Unfortunately for Jacqueline, I had no idea what her sodium was and no way to find out, so I guessed. I used three-quarter-normal saline with some additional potassium which gave a margin for error either way. Within two days, Jacqueline made the transition from near death to a skinny but hungry infant who in a month became chubby, cute and smiling.

I treated hundreds of patients like Jacqueline and became competent at handling dehydration. I remembered the advice of Dr. Sharbaugh, who cared for dehydrated babies for forty years. He never checked electrolytes; "a waste of money" he said. All that was needed was to hydrate the baby until the diarrhea stopped and keep the baby in the hospital until the urine was free of ketones. Although I did not exactly agree, I at least found Dr. Sharbaugh's advice consoling.

But Dr. Sharbaugh was right. I never did see any of the feared complications of electrolyte imbalance; however, I quickly learned that if I gave too much fluid, the consequences were devastating.

As soon as I walked into the Children's Home, I noticed Carmel was in trouble. She had arrived the day before with malnutrition and dehydration from diarrhea. But now, she was breathing too rapidly. Suspecting pneumonia, I asked the mother if her child was having fevers. She was not. Placing my stethoscope on her chest gave me the diagnosis. To my horror, I heard rales emanating from her lungs. They were filled with fluid. Why? Because I had put it there.

I checked the intravenous rate. It was the appropriate amount. Perhaps she was in kidney failure and could not excrete urine or maybe the rate had been higher previously. The reason did not matter. Carmel was now in fulminant heart failure.

Having never treated heart failure in a child, I retreated to my pediatric textbook. It was simple; just like adults except that the doses were smaller. All I had to do was give oxygen; Digoxin, a drug that strengthens the heart's contractions; and a diuretic, which causes the kidneys to excrete urine at a faster rate.

There were several problems. The Children's Home had no Digoxin or oxygen; however, there was a powerful diuretic called Lasix. I gave it intravenously, knowing that in twenty minutes at the latest, Carmel would urinate, eliminating the excess fluid, relieving the strain on her weak heart, enabling it to more efficiently clear the lungs of excess fluid. Ten, fifteen, twenty minutes; no urine and still breathing at a rate of 60 per minute. Not panicking, I doubled the dose of Lasix, confidently expecting the urine to pour out. Nothing. I placed a catheter in her bladder; still nothing.

With her ribs rising and falling 60 times a minute, she gazed at me with a blank mindless expression that intimated, "You are losing me." Trying to remain calm while watching a unnecessary death, I was struck with another possibility; perhaps the Lasix was expired. Checking the container confirmed my suspicion; the Lasix had expired three years ago and was no longer effective.

I gave her another large dose anyway, and jumped on my moped to obtain some unexpired Lasix from Sans Fil. Upon returning, I saw

Carmel propped up and dressed in her Sunday best, a pressed pink shirt with white shorts. The sisters have great respect for the dead. Seeing the dejection on my face, one of the sisters tried to console me by saying that Carmel came here to die. I did not argue, but I knew her death was "iatrogenic," a fancy medical word for treatment-induced. As I watched the sisters lovingly place her body in a cardboard box, I thought of the old cliché, "Accountants erase their mistakes, doctors bury theirs."

Her death reflected the inherent danger in treating a malnourished child for dehydration under inadequate supervision. These children needed to be observed constantly for the signs of fluid overload – increased respiratory rate, rales, faster heart beat and edema. At night, this was impossible. The sisters had to sleep and so did I. After Carmel's death, I stopped the intravenous lines every evening, unless the dehydration was still life-threatening. Adding fluid was much easier than removing it.

I had to be careful not to rehydrate these infants too rapidly. In a healthy American child, the heart can tolerate the rapid fluid load so that the child can be rehydrated in several hours. In Haiti, this was not possible; a gradual infusion was needed. Malnourished children permitted no mistakes. If I made one, they died.

I was constantly treating dehydration. The diarrhea that caused it spread rapidly because the Children's Home was a health inspector's nightmare. The Haitian women hired to clean and feed the children had no concept of sanitation. I never saw one wash her hands. Even if they were so inclined, there was no running water. At feeding time, the women would break up avocadoes and go from child to child, shoving the pieces into each mouth with their filthy hands. I cringed as I thought of the hordes of bacteria being transferred by the spreading saliva. When a child vomited, the women instinctively tried to catch the vomit. I never understood why, because most of it fell on the floor anyway. When they changed the diapers, they would also use the soiled diaper as a rag and residual fecal material got on their hands. Then they would go to prepare the food.

Upon my arrival, I continuously tried to change these habits, telling them they were spreading disease. They stared at me blankly. The germ theory was news to them.

Eventually I realized that trying to change them was a losing battle. The ranting of a blan doctor who barely spoke Creole could not modify ages of cultural habits. I grudgingly accepted it and dealt with it the best I could while watching the diarrhea spread from bed to bed.

Another frustrating aspect of working in Haiti was the complications and deaths I saw from lack of equipment. Many of those who died, no one could help, but sometimes there was a child who could benefit from the superior laboratory facilities found in a hospital setting. Unfortunately, even these children died when I sent them to a hospital. Only one ever returned to the Children's Home.

Charles was a two-year-old with total body swelling who I diagnosed as having kidney failure when I noticed he was not making urine. His body could no longer maintain the proper electrolyte concentrations, making death inevitable. There are three treatments – a kidney transplant, dialysis or prayer. I was employing the latter.

It was not working. Charles continued to make little urine and one day I noticed his eyes bobbing upward as if he were trying to look over his shoulder. His right arm and leg were flexing at the same frequency and his previously alert face was expressionless. Charles was having a seizure.

Rummaging through the medicines, I found some Valium and administered it intravenously. The seizure continued. Next I tried some expired Dilantin – no change. Finally, using Phenobarbital, I stopped the seizure.

Suspecting the cause to be electrolyte imbalance, I had him taken to a hospital. This was not one of my better moves. There he was placed in a bed for a month and nobody watched him except for the women the sisters sent to bring him food. He must have been totally ignored because every time I visited him, he was having another seizure. Eventually, the continuous seizures caused brain damage and he lapsed into a semicomatose state, rarely moving and responding only to painful stimuli.

When he returned to the Children's Home, he was a complete disaster. Because he was always supine, huge bedsores had developed on his head and back, infected by his own feces in which he had been lying. Even worse, his limbs were frozen. Once a patient is comatose, the muscles contract from disuse. It is like getting rigor mortis before dying. Only intensive physical therapy prevents this. Poor Charles now had his arms permanently flexed so he looked like a begging dog. Later he contracted pneumonia and died.

Care like this is not unique to Haiti. American nursing home care is often of similar quality unless the patient can afford tens of thousands of dollars annually. When I saw Charles's state, I told the sisters that unless we were willing to pay for private care – which was available in Haiti – there was no sense in sending a child to a hospital. They could die just as well with us.

Just because death was common, it did not make it easier to take. One day when I walked into the Children's Home, one of the sisters asked me to see a baby that had just arrived. The sisters had started an intravenous line but the baby showed no response.

The mother looked at me and said, "Li dekonpoze", "She has become unresponsive."

She was right. The baby, a ten-month old girl, lay in the crib with her mouth and eyes half open and the faceless expression of a statue, reflecting a brain that was functioning on primitive reflexes. She breathed at random intervals – sometimes in couplets, other times taking twenty seconds between each breath. As she inspired, her chest rose slowly, accompanied by a slight flare of her nostrils. At the peak of each inspiration her lips oscillated, as if she were taking a few quick gasps to get more oxygen, even though her lungs had reached maximum expansion. Then began a slow decrescendo, her chest falling and a faint warble emanating from her throat as the ejecting air played her vocal cords.

I rubbed my knuckles sharply against her breast bone, feeling in my bones her rapidly beating heart. She had no response to this noxious stimulus. I picked up her white cadaverous hand – with red painted fingernails – and dropped it. It fell like a rock, at the same speed the acceleration of gravity would permit – lifeless, with no muscle tone from the arm to impede its descent. Her pupils did not budge when I flashed my penlight into her eyes.

While her spirit watched me from above, I gave her a bolus of bicarbonate, hoping to normalize the acid concentration in her blood. Both of us knew I was wasting my time, treating my psychological well-being rather than admit my impotence in reversing the irreversible. Nothing happened, nor should it have had. Rather than search for another drug I stopped, and just watched along with the sisters who had seen this scenario often, but like me, never got used to watching senseless deaths.

The crescendo-decrescendo continued for another five minutes. Then urine began to come from her urethra. It did not arc into the air, but trickled slowly in between her labia, and mixed with the watery greenish-brown feces that had begun to ooze out of her rectum. Her bladder and intestinal muscles were relaxing from their state of constant tone during life.

I continued to watch, waiting for the next crescendo-decrescendo. It never came. There was no premordial final gasp, no gaping of the mouth with outstretched arms and blazing eyes, no noble attempt to continue existing. The breathing simply stopped. I placed my stethoscope on her chest, listening to stillness – the deafening sound of silence. The feces continued to ooze from her rectum.

The mother was glancing at me apprehensively, trying to read my face. She was 18, a handsome woman with high cheekbones, a white polka-dot red handkerchief tied around her head, and a full length white and yellow plaid dress. This was her first child.

There is no good way to tell someone that a loved one has died. Hoping to avoid it, I walked away. Physicians try to be calm and compassionate in this situation, but it does not dull the pain. As an intern, it had been my job to relay this information, but I never got good at it and probably never will. Regaining my confidence, I returned and did what had to be done.

"Madanm, li mouri", "Madam, she's dead", I said tenderly.

Her expression did not change. She just glanced away from me and changed the baby's diaper, neatly tying the knots on the baby's limp body. Then she took a bottle and placed it in her baby's mouth. The nipple only displaced the lips so she opened the teeth and pushed the nipple inside. She held the bottle for a moment then looked at me with pleading eyes saying, "Doktè, li pa bwè", "Doctor, she would not drink." Holding back my tears and unsuccessfully trying to keep my voice from choking, I responded, "M' regrèt, madanm, li mouri", "I'm sorry, Madam, she's dead."

She stood there for about ten seconds, although it seemed longer. I watched her closely. Suddenly, she fell to the floor and screamed. "Ooyyee" reverberated through the Children's Home. She kicked and thrashed on the floor until some Haitian women comforted her and gave her some water. I stood there dazed and then left and played with some of the healthy children.

The sisters took the children's bodies to a mortuary beside the Hôpital Général. One day, while in a masochistic mood, I decided to go with them. It was a one-story building, conveniently located near the Depot.

When I walked in, molecules of decomposing flesh invaded my nostrils. This visceral stench was like a hard right hook to my head, momentarily staggering me. I was not used to this smell because dead bodies in the United States are preserved with formaldehyde, which has an overpowering odor itself.

The room looked like the inside of a factory warehouse, with concrete floors and decaying lifeless walls. To the left were stacks of pine boxes. Beside them were large vaults with steel doors stacked in two layers, with five in each row. Overhanging the room was an air compressor emitting an ominous low rumble, an introductory drum roll for what I was about to see.

I carried in a box with a dead child and gave it to a waiting young man who then proceeded to go about his job like a service station attendant pumping gas. He opened one of the steel doors. To my concealed horror, several dead babies spewed onto the floor. Their limbs were pliable indicating they had died in the past several hours; rigor mortis had not set in yet. The young man, with an irritated look on his face, grabbed the bodies, shoved them back into the vault and forced the door shut.

He moved to the next vault and opened the door. Inside lay a pile of dead babies, their limbs randomly arranged with little arms and legs poking out in all directions. They had cotton stuffed in their mouths and were twisted in unnatural positions. One baby had its head rotated 180 degrees, so that I could see both its buttocks and blank face looking through me. The man tossed our delivery on top of the heap, making a dull thud as it settled on the collective amorphous humanity below. I quit work for the day and retreated to a bar in Pétionville to support the local brewery.

What kept me going was the lives I did save. Louisa was a three-year-old who, according to her mother, suddenly developed difficulty breathing two days previously. Louisa sat in front of me, leaning forward, her shoulders rapidly rising and falling. With each breath, a harsh whistle came from her throat–stridor in medical parlance. Saliva drooled from each corner of her mouth, dripping onto her thighs. She wanted to cry, but was afraid to, afraid of compromising the little oxygen she was getting.

I stared at her, thinking to myself, "I should know what this is." She stared back, instinctively grasping that I was the key player in her future existence, almost as if she could hear the index cards flipping through my brain. When I came to the right one, the words of my pediatrics professor echoed through my mind, "I don't want even those of you going into psychiatry to forget this diagnosis." It was the classic presentation of a life-threatening disease, epiglottitis.

The epiglottis is a circular piece of tissue that covers the trachea, or windpipe, and prevents the aspiration of food into the lungs while swallowing. When infected, it increases in size, partially occluding the windpipe and resulting in air hunger. Since swallowing will block the trachea even more, the patient wisely opts to let the saliva drip out.

Since Louisa could not drink, I started an intravenous line so she would not become dehydrated and also for the antibiotics, Ampicillin and Chloramphenicol. My main fear was that she would develop complete obstruction of the trachea, forcing me to cut a hole into it through her neck – a prospect I did not relish. Fortunately, Louisa responded beautifully. After a sleepless night during which she refused to lie down, the stridor stopped, as did her drooling. It took several days before she had the courage to eat and I continued the intravenous antibiotics for a week. Soon she was exploring the Children's Home, but eventually left with her mother, after the sisters fattened her up.

Some children got better even though I never made a diagnosis. One girl, Chantal, was brought to the door by her desperate mother. Limp and lifeless, she lay in her mother's arms about to meet her maker. Quickly, I placed her in a bed and examined her, noting her ice cold hands and feet. Her pulse was too fast to count, at least 180 beats per minute. Chantal was in shock, a state in which the body shunts blood to the most important organs – the heart, brain and kidneys – and ignores the rest. Her pale brown skin contrasted the coal black color of her mother – indicating anemia as well.

Another child in Haiti was about to die. Placing a tourniquet on her right arm, I searched for a vein to start an intravenous line. Nothing popped up. I checked the left arm – nothing. With scissors and razor flying, I partially shaved her scalp, accidently making some small cuts that hardly bled. I tightly placed the tourniquet around her head and out of nowhere popped this huge vein. I positioned her like a sack of wheat so that I was comfortable. She did not whimper or even budge as the needle impaled her translucent skin.

Within five minutes of my seeing her, normal saline was pouring into her veins, but she also needed something else. If a body in shock is not getting enough oxygen, it switches to anaerobic – without oxygen – metabolism. This gift from our evolutionary ancestors provides temporary, perhaps life-saving energy, but it also produces acid by-products which poison the heart. This acid is neutralized by giving bicarbonate and therefore bicarbonate is one of the first drugs administered in a patient whose heart has just stopped.

Since I did not have a costly machine to measure acid concentration, I did not know how much bicarbonate to give so I just guessed, plugging hypothetical numbers into a memorized formula and arriving at the dosage. Bicarbonate rarely works because it does not address the cause of the shock, whether it be rampant infection or fluid loss. Nonetheless, I drew some up in a syringe in my usual non-sterile fashion that made visiting volunteer nurses cringe, and injected it.

For some reason, it worked. It was like Lazarus coming back from the dead. Within seconds, Chantal started to thrash around, screaming and kicking, upset that I had rudely interrupted her death. As with all children, her hand instinctively went to her head to pull out the disturbing needle sticking in her scalp. My hands instinctively stopped her and three minutes later, we had a howling, gyrating two-year old tied down in a barbaric but effective fashion. Guessing again at the dosage, I added bicarbonate to the normal saline solution, insuring that she would receive a slow constant infusion to maintain the proper acid concentration while her body slowly compensated. This is exactly what happened; her feet and hands warmed up, tears welled-up in her eyes and her mother began chanting some prayer that I could not understand but I am sure the sisters approved because it sounded Catholic.

Her long term care was more challenging. I never determined why she was in shock in spite of several spinal taps, multiple malaria checks and microscopic examination of every secretion. She never had a fever, but in Haiti this is not significant, because the patients are so sick and malnourished that they can not mount one. Just to be safe, I gave her a week of intravenous antibiotics.

Chantal would not eat for two weeks but managed to fight when I passed a nasogastric tube through her nose into her stomach. With it, she got her nutrition and the protracted recuperative process began, first with her nibbling her food and then developing a hearty appetite. Her cheeks fattened, her belly grew and she began to stand up and ambulate. Her brown skin turned ebony as the anemia corrected. Eventually, she started smiling, running around and playing with the toys. She especially enjoyed playing with the miniature plastic bricks, stacking them up and gleefully knocking themover. Her mother was so pleased she offered to give me Chantel as payment. Perhaps she also knew that when she took her Chantel home, her daughter would soon be sick again.

The most pathetic patient in the Children's Home was a four-year-old girl, Alice. When I first saw her, she had a well-demarcated rash on her face, arms and upper legs. This disfigurement made her a pariah, forcing her to stand away from the other children to avoid their cruel teasing. I did not know what the rash was, but I assumed its cause was fungal and started treating her with an expired anti-fungal medicine. Not only did she not improve; she got worse. Bewildered, I had no alternate plan of therapy until a visiting dermatologist came to my rescue.

Andrew Simone was prospering in his six-figure private practice in Toronto when he discovered he was not happy. A short, roly-poly balding man, he was of Italian descent and looked it. His bearded face and humble demeanor gave one the impression he was a monk rather than a physician. In his search for spiritual well-being, Andrew donated all his earthly possessions to the poor. He continued to work, but he gave his income to the poor, too. He fed his wife and nine children by asking for donations. Begging, he claimed, kept him humble and able to empathize with the poor.

Many who met Andrew felt he was unhinged, but he was not. He just responded to the rat race in a productive manner rather than becoming an alcoholic or regressing to a second adolescence like so many others. There was one thing Andrew was – a crackerjack dermatologist. Harvard-trained and gifted with a phenomenal memory, Andrew taught me the dermatology of blacks. I had tried to learn some of this subspeciality by reading on my own, but the civil rights movement has yet to make it to dermatology textbooks; the pictures are of Caucasians. With Andrew's help, I learned to diagnosis leprosy, syphilis, sarcoidosis, tuberculosis, psoriasis, scabies and eczema.

But Alice baffled even Andrew. He had never seen anything like it. We tried antibiotics, vitamin creams, steroid creams, anti-fungal potions and holy water. Nothing worked. Poor Alice developed huge amorphous concretions around her eyelids and cheeks, a hideous raccoon-like mask that made her appear extraterrestial. They spread down her back, arms and to her hands, protruding from her fingernails like rhinoceros horns. These concretions cracked apart and bled, making them exquisitely painful. Alice's very existence was torture. She howled when anyone touched her, totally rejecting human warmth. The emotional scars were as devastating as the physical ones.

I took every doctor who stopped at the Children's Home to see Alice. Nobody knew her diagnosis, but the cameras clicked. One day, the long-awaited phone call came. An oncologist from Texas showed the pictures of Alice to his colleagues, who concluded that a biopsy was needed to make the diagnosis. They offered to examine the biopsy and send the necessary medicine free of charge.

I hung up the phone, finished the most urgent work and then hopped on my moped, shopping from pharmacy to pharmacy for two hours until finding one that carried the preservative formalin. Returning to the Children's Home, I found the instruments needed to perform a biopsy. Alice always had the same reaction to my presence – unadulterated terror – since I often caused pain by applying my latest ineffective potion. This was even worse. I anesthetized her right forearm and excised an ample piece of pathological tissue and placed it in the formalin. The next day it was on its way to Texas.

One month later, another doctor arrived from Texas with the diagnosis, "Mucocutaneous Candidiasis" – a fungal infection. I had never heard of this entity, but the doctor was kind enough to bring several journal articles, too, and these I quickly devoured. More important, he gave me a powerful but expensive antifungal drug to administer to Alice twice a day. Each pill cost two dollars.

It worked. The concretions dried up and fell, leaving a mild rash. Alice began to smile and play with the other children. She even allowed me to hold her, although she always eyed me suspiciously.

Between the deaths and patients like Alice and Chantal, my moods swung from depression to euphoria, rarely I experienced anything in-between. The sickness of a child is grossly unfair. Even the most hardened of individuals can not stand to see a child suffer. An ill adult understands what illness is, but all a child comprehends is its miserable state. A child will cry, refuse to eat and ignore human warmth. It was in the Children's Home that I learned it is truly the children who suffer.

Haitian mother with her two children. The infant she is holding has kwashiorkor (page 92). Note the infant's pale skin color and light hair when compared to her sister and mother.

Haitian family with child suffering from marasmus(page 91). He is emaciated but strong enough to complain – a good sign.

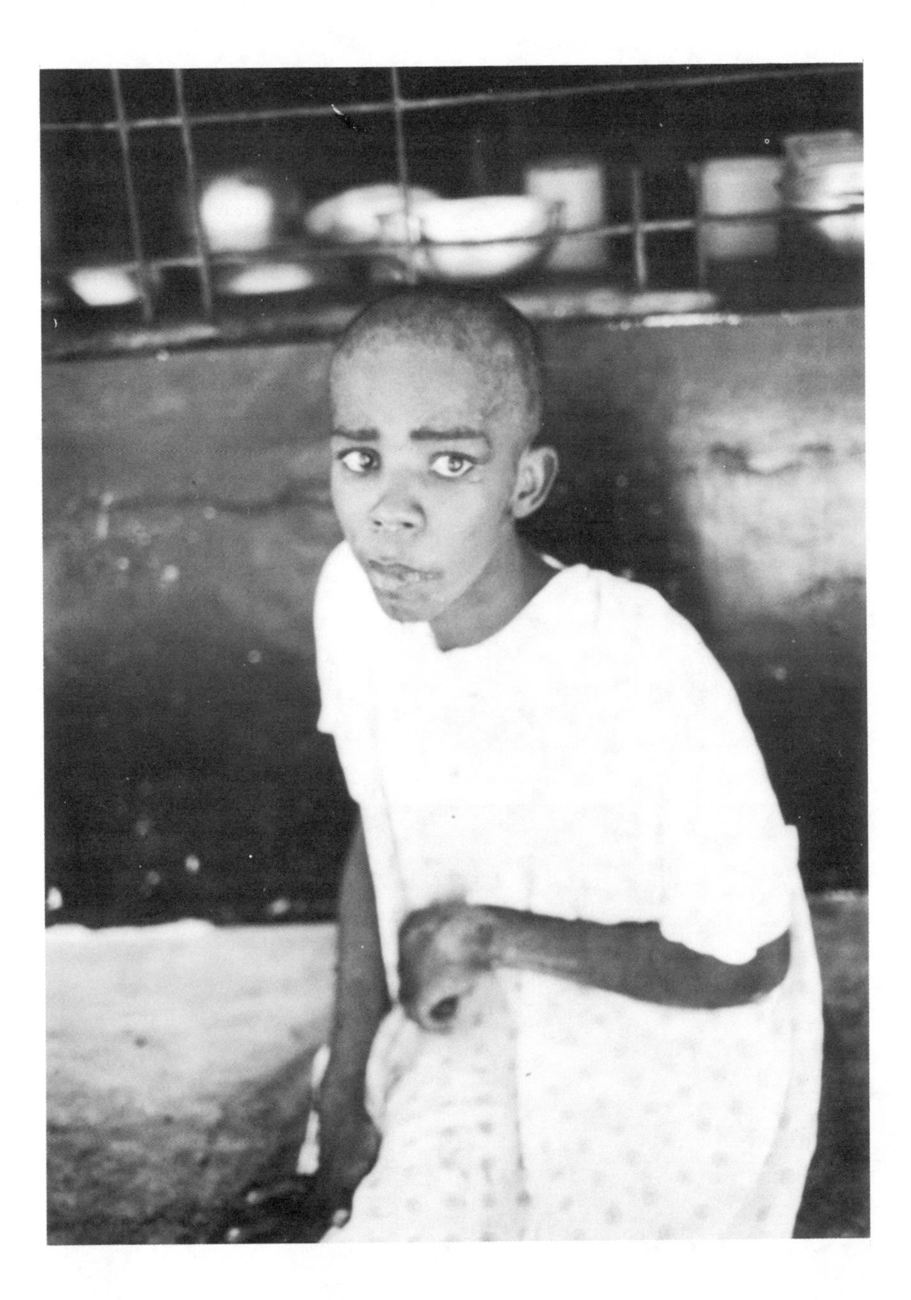

Partially paralyzed young man at Sans Fil. His head is shaven because of a scabies infestation (page 80).

Elda (page 76), who eventually died from tuberculosis.

Pierre (page 146), the sage of Sans Fil.

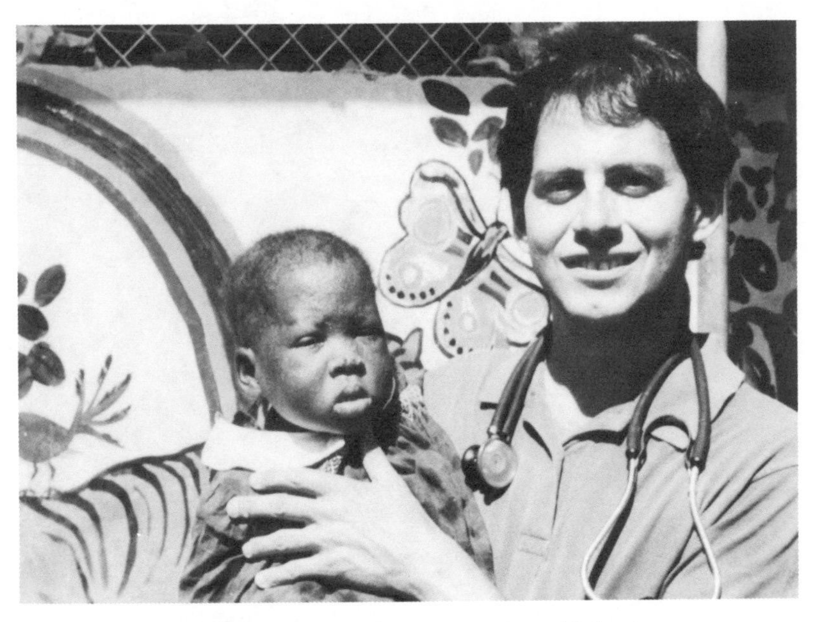

Alice (page 68), recovering from a rare fungal infection.

Chapter 5

The Water is Filthy and There's No Place to Live

Kay koule tronpe solèy, men li pa tronpe lapli.
The house that leaks can fool the sun but not fool the rain.

Haitian proverb

The sisters were perplexed by Ricardo's condition. Although being treated for tuberculosis, he languished – a two-year-old tipping the scales at 15 pounds – underweight even by Haitian standards. Ricardo was a beautiful child with curly brown hair and bronzed skin. As his mother was jet black, I suspected his father was either white or mulatto. Ricardo never smiled, and howled in pure terror whenever I approached him. Having exhausted all therapeutic options, I gave him a blood transfusion.

Within two days, he developed a ravenous appetite, gobbling every morsel within reach and howling until he received more food. Several weeks later, he was an ebullient twenty-five-pounder, jumping about his crib, and scrutinizing everyone who entered the Children's Home. He always recognized me, pointing his finger at me while yelling a distinctive gibberish and laughing uproariously when I tickled him. He had forgiven me for sticking needles into his arms and pushing tubes down his throat. He was so popular that the sisters allowed him to stay an extra month. Eventually, his mother took him back to her home.

One month later, the mother was in a food line without Ricardo. When asked, she sullenly reported that Ricardo had developed diarrhea and died. The sisters were devastated, one of them confiding in me that she questioned the sense of her mission. She had spent several sleepless nights keeping Ricardo alive. Unfortunately, Ricardo's story was typical.

The day will come when policy makers realize that no number of doctors can eradicate diseases without addressing the underlying conditions that precipitate them. The number of faucets in a country is a more accurate health indicator than the number of doctors. Medicine can not solve social problems. When 12 people live in a one-room house, using the same cup to drink water that comes from a well that contains raw sewage, no amount of medicine will prevent rampant illnesses. Because of poor housing and abysmal sanitation, typhoid, tuberculosis, worms, scabies and hepatitis were at epidemic proportions. Failure to drain Haiti's swamps made malaria rampant.

The biggest killer was tuberculosis. Before coming to Haiti, I had seen two cases, but here I saw thousands. Half the patients at Sans Fil were afflicted by it. Before antibiotics, tuberculosis was greatly feared in the United States. Those who contracted it had fewer rights than a rapist and were sentenced to sanitoriums. Upon seeing its complications, I understood why.

Theresa Louis, an attractive thirty-year-woman, eked out her livelihood selling food at the market near the Children's Home. For over a month she had had a cough accompanied by high fevers and difficulty breathing. She ignored these problems until one day while spitting, a habit of Haitian women, she saw fresh blood in her sputum. This brought her to me.

Her diagnosis was straight forward, as she had the common signs of tuberculosis – anemia, enlarged lymph nodes, clubbing of her fingers and fluid in her lungs. I confirmed it by examining her sputum under the microscope and seeing the characteristic bacteria. She was taken to Sans Fil and placed on anti-tuberculosis medicine. Within two weeks her lungs were free of fluid and the fevers stopped. She returned to her job at the market, continuing her medicine.

Four months later, I was walking near the Children's Home when I heard a woman shouting, "Doktè Joe, Doktè Joe." The Haitians called me this, as my surname was unpronounceable. I immediately recognized Theresa Louis. Wearing a flowing green dress with a red bandanna, she was more beautiful than I remembered. I grabbed her tightly and kissed her on the cheek. She was proof I was helping someone. I asked her if she still took her medicine, something she adamantly confirmed, showing me her pills. She made small talk, graciously complimenting me on my improved Creole and asking how long I planned to stay in Haiti. I bought some peanut brittle from her thirteen-year-old daughter, giving her a gourde. Theresa Louis presented me with the appropriate change. Because I had cared for her, she did not overcharge me, even though she saw me pull thirty dollars, a small fortune, out of my pocket.

Not all cases of tuberculosis had such a happy ending. The causative bacteria are spread by the respiratory route and expelled into the air with each cough. Entire families, especially when debilitated by malnutrition, become infected. Haitians exacerbate the problem by closing the windows and doors of their crowded domiciles at night to keep out evil spirits. The stigma of tuberculosis prevents many patients from seeking health care, as it is assumed they have broken God's laws to deserve such a fate.

Blacks, unlike whites, have poor natural resistance to tuberculosis. Whites have lived with this disease for millennia and a strong immunity has evolved. Blacks, on the other hand, first encountered tuberculosis when they were enslaved five hundred years ago. Untreated chronic tuberculosis may fester in a white for years, even decades, but it kills a black in a matter of months.

Tuberculosis starts in the lungs because the bacillus is "aerobic" – oxygen-requiring. Once established, it proceeds to render the patient miserable with an annoying cough. As it progresses, the infection erodes through blood vessels and the patient coughs up blood, like Theresa Louis. It destroys lung tissue and causes the lungs to fill with fluid, resulting in shortness of breath. The fevers begin in the late afternoon, and break during sleep, accompanied by profuse sweating. Appetite is diminished and the patient rapidly loses weight. If attacked early, tuberculosis can be contained to the lungs; if not, any organ is fair game – the kidneys, skin, brain, eyes and even the heart.

Tuberculosis patients become anemic because their debilitated state prevents the bone marrow from making enough red blood cells. When I first arrived I quantified the anemia by using a "Hemoglobinometer," a device that determines the concentration of red blood cells in blood. I quickly discarded it when I learned to estimate the severity of the anemia just as accurately by examining the patient. The skin, even in blacks, becomes pale, especially in the creases on the palms of the hands. The inside of the eyelid, the conjunctiva, turns from its usual red to white. Routinely, I saw tuberculosis patients whose black skin had turned to white, an anemia so severe that it was barely compatible with life.

The only way to definitively diagnose tuberculosis is to culture the causative bacillus on agar. Since my laboratory was poorly equipped, I employed the second best test, a microscopic examination of the patient's sputum. The patient had to cough hard so that the sputum came from the lungs. Getting saliva from only the mouth was useless. The sample was then smeared on a glass slide and allowed to dry. After application of several stains on a specimen, the tuberculosis bacteria appeared bright red in an iridescent blue background. This test also could be employed on other body fluids, such as fecal material, spinal fluid and pus.

Another test for tuberculosis was a "PPD" skin test – "purified protein derivative" – and is a part of the actual tuberculosis bacillus. When a patient has an exposure to tuberculosis, the body responds by making antibodies to combat it. After the infection is eradicated, the body retains the ability to manufacture these antibodies rapidly if reinfected. When a PPD is injected under the skin, these antibodies attack, resulting in the skin around the injected site to become red and elevated. This test is used to screen pre-schoolers in the United States.

At first, I thought the PPD would be an ideal test for diagnosing tuberculosis, but soon I found it to be worthless. Everyone in Haiti had been exposed, so everyone had a positive PPD. One woman's arm puffed up like the Michelin tire man; it did not exactly inspire her to have much confidence in my ability. The only patients with a negative PPD were those with endstage tuberculosis who were too sick to manufacture antibodies.

Treating tuberculosis was more challenging. It is an art in itself, requiring a careful history of previous therapy along with an intensive effort to educate the patient in the anti-tuberculosis regimen. Health personnel in the third world have developed various protocols, reducing the misery of tuberculosis until improvement in the economic conditions allows suitable housing and sanitation to contain it.

The first line of attack is to administer two drugs so that if the bacteria evolve resistance to one the other is still available. In Haiti and most of the Third World, these drugs are Isoniazid and Thiacetazone. They are inexpensive, Isoniazid costing only 1 cent a pill and Thiacetazone available for much less, 100 pills for 1 cent. The cost of saving a life is only $4.00.

Unfortunately, there is a catch. Thiacetazone is a lethal drug, killing almost 1% of people because it causes a hideous allergic reaction, Stevens-Johnson syndrome. From a public health point of view though, Thiacetazone saves more than it kills. It is the only anti-tuberculosis drug the Third-World poor can afford, so it is either Thiacetazone or nothing.

However, I found public health semantics to be of little comfort when one of my patients died each week from Stevens-Johnson syndrome. First the skin would begin to bubble up, covering the patient with welts from the face to the feet. These welts then burst and the skin literally peeled off the patient's body, exposing a raw, bleeding, painful layer of subcutaneous tissue. Meanwhile, the lips and eyelids ballooned, rendering the face into an amorphous orb of featureless raw skin. The patient is now blind, unable to eat or drink and in such pain that any movement is torture. Haitians are not complainers, and the patients afflicted with this horror accepted it with a quiet dignity until an inevitable infection killed them.

In the United States Stevens-Johnson syndrome has a 15% mortality, but in Haiti it was 100%. Initially, I worked hard trying to save these patients, but it was an exercise in futility. I administered the proper treatment – intravenous hydration, antibiotics, steroids and nutrition via a nasogastric tube. They still died. These patients also needed constant nursing care involving meticulous wound care with sterile technique, turning to prevent bedsores and constant reassurance.

This I could not do.

What I could do was replace Thiacetazone with another pill, Ethambutol. Although more expensive, it combined with Isoniazid produced many cures with few side effects. It was gratifying to see my etiolated anemic coughing patients become healthy in a few months.

Then the real battle begins. Tuberculosis patients have to take medicine for a year after they feel fine. The tuberculosis has not been eradicated, only beaten back and plotting to return at the least opportunity with the vengeance of an army that has lost the battle but has no intention of losing the war. Even educated patients rarely take medicine when they have no complaints. This is the reason public service advertisements urge those with high blood pressure to comply with their treatment. High blood pressure has few symptoms until the patient has had a devastating stroke or heart attack. Until that time, few people see any sense in disciplining themselves to take an annoying pill four times a day, especially if it has side effects.

Talking Haitians who feel healthy into taking medicine that can consume 10% of their income is impossible. Therefore, the sisters devised a clever system to encourage compliance; they not only gave the medicine free but also bribed them. Every week, when the patients returned to get their medicine, they also received food and milk. Even if they saw no sense in returning just to get pills prescribed by some crazy blan doctor, there definitely was merit to getting free food. I reinforced the need to take the pills, explaining they still had tuberculosis and failure to comply would mean death. I was not exaggerating. Haiti was full of people with partially-treated tuberculosis and when it recurred the cheap drugs no longer worked. They required the big guns – Streptomycin and Rifamptin – and if these were unavailable, they died. Naturally, these drugs were expensive, especially Rifamptin, which cost 50 cents for a daily dose. Nobody donated this drug. When visitors asked what I needed, I always replied "Rifamptin." People offered to donate electrocardiogram machines, surgical instruments and other worthless items. I replied, "I want Rifamptin." Finally, Andrew Simone pulled several thousand dollars out his own pocket and purchased the drug.

I wrestled with drug-resistant tuberculosis daily. Elda was a perfect example. She had been treated three times with assorted drug regimens including Rifamptin and Streptomycin. As soon as symptoms abated, she did not bother to continue her medicine. Now she was at Sans Fil and her fevers and cough continued, no matter what

I tried. Finally she left, telling me she was going to try a combination of milk and orange juice, one of Haiti's many folk remedies. I did not argue, since it could not be any less effective than my treatment. One month later, I was rounding at the Depot when I heard "Doktè Joe, Doktè Joe." When I turned around, there was poor Elda, lying on the ground. When she had left Sans Fil, I thought it would be impossible for her to lose more weight. I was wrong. Elda was literally a living skeleton with her taut skin stretched across her prominent ribs and cheekbones. Her arms and legs were so wasted I could identify the individual bones. This is why the old textbooks called tuberculosis consumption. Even well-nourished, Elda would not have been attractive, which is why she had earned her living begging instead of by prostitution.

"M' ap mouri", "I'm dying," she informed me. Knowing I could not save her, she only asked me to bring her to Sans Fil and let her die in a bed. Before placing her in the Depot, the doctors at the Hôpital Général had taken a chest X-ray. Her entire lung field was covered with small oval white flecks, each representing a pocket of pus. Elda had "miliary" tuberculosis, so-called because the white flecks look like millet seeds. The most feared complication, it means that the tuberculosis has entered the blood stream and spread through the body. Treatment was futile.

In spite of her condition Elda and I had a friendly chat, but by the time the sisters took her to Sans Fil, she had irreversibly deteriorated. She surrendered her spirit when she knew she could die in bed. She no longer recognized me, ranting and shrieking incoherently. When I asked the other women what she was saying, one replied, "Li gen tèt cho", "She's crazy." Either she had tuberculosis meningitis or her blood pressure was too low to perfuse her brain. I pharmacologically comforted her with a liberal dose of Valium, allowing a peaceful death several hours later.

The key to curing tuberculosis was an accurate history of previous therapy. For example, a patient may have had an incomplete course of Isoniazid and Thiacetazone at a rural missionary before moving to Port-au-Prince. Two years later, the cough and fevers return and he comes to our clinic. Chances are his case is resistant to Isoniazid and Thiacetazone, so I had to choose two other drugs such as Ethambutol and Rifamptin – when available. If he failed to complete this course, he would end up like Elda. To my surprise, the

Haitians knew the names of the medicine they had taken. Occasionally, a patient had forgotten but I could find out by quizzing him on the color of the pills.

Tuberculosis caused a slow death like cancer and made the patient miserable by impairing breathing. One man at Sans Fil, Eugene, had tuberculosis but otherwise seemed healthy, with good muscle bulk and a hearty appetite. However, he was breathing too rapidly. When I listened to his lungs, the right side had normal breath sounds, but on the left side I heard nothing. Using percussion, I ascertained the right side was full of air but the left side sounded dull. The left lung cavity was filled with fluid, a pleural effusion, a frequent complication in tuberculosis. The best treatment is to ignore it, since it will resorb as the underlying disease is cured; however, this man's effusion was huge and making him uncomfortable. It had to be removed.

The procedure to remove a pleural effusion is called a thorocentesis. First one obtains a chest X-ray to confirm the diagnosis and then drains the fluid by inserting a needle into the lung cavity. The danger is that the needle can puncture the lung – lethal in a patient with severe lung disease. Consequently, I approached Eugene with caution and trepidation, especially since I had no X-ray equipment and was relying entirely on physical examination. In the United States, this would be considered gross malpractice.

Fortunately for Eugene, I had done many thorocenteses as an intern and had no difficulty hitting the effusion. I stuck an angiocath directly above one of the lower left ribs and pulled out the stylet, leaving only a plastic catheter in the lung cavity. This prevented puncturing of the lung as it reexpanded. Twenty minutes and three quarts of fluid later, Eugene was breathing easier and thanking me profusely. Thorocentesis became so routine at Sans Fil that I soon had Day and Nick doing them. Nonetheless, visiting doctors raised their eyebrows when they saw one of us plunge a needle into a patient's chest without the benefit of an X-ray.

When I first arrived in Haiti, I would not subject a patient to the potential side effects of anti-tuberculosis medicine unless I espied the bright red bacillus under the microscope. But when I witnessed the suffering this disease caused, I changed. Any patient who had a cough and fever for over a month had tuberculosis until proven otherwise. If

I heard wheezes in the lungs, felt an enlarged neck lymph node or saw clubbing of the fingers, I started the medicine. It was impractical to look at the sputum of all tuberculosis suspects. Dozens of diseases such as lung cancer, sarcoidosis or fungal infections had similar symptoms, but I lacked medicine to treat them. Thus I rationalized that the sin of omission was worse than giving anti-tuberculosis medicine to a few patients who did not have the disease.

This represented a complete reversal of my medical philosophy. American physicians are trained to have a diagnosis before giving treatment. There is nothing worse than causing a nasty side effect with an unnecessary medicine. Also, starting a medicine prematurely can obscure a diagnosis. For example, treating a patient with antibiotics makes it more difficult to culture the causative organism. But in Haiti, all the rules changed. The best test was to see if the patient responded to the medicine.

Nowhere was this truer than with the children. Many were like Marie Helena, who was losing weight and having fevers for no apparent reason. I had examined her multiple times, failing to find a cause. Then I randomly tried various antibiotics with lackluster results. I even treated her for malaria, although I never saw the causative parasites in her blood. The fevers continued. After exhausting all possibilities, I only had one thought remaining, tuberculosis. I managed to obtain a chest X-ray from one of the local hospitals, but it was normal. I even put a nasogastric tube into her stomach several times, examining the aspirate for the characteristic bright red bacillus.

Even in distress, Marie Helena was a gorgeous child. With her cover-girl chocolate skin and curly black hair, she was the darling of the Children's Home. She had the most toys in her crib and there were polite discussions among the visitors over who should feed her. One visiting doctor practically adopted her – feeding her, changing her, dressing her, photographing her – everything but figuring out what was wrong with her.

Finally, I bit the bullet and treated her for tuberculosis. She did not even have a cough. Within a day, her appetite improved and soon, Marie Helena was eating like a little pig. The fevers stopped and she became even cuter, something I did not think was possible. With some meat on her bones, she was a true prima donna, a corpulent, temperamental darling pampered by all. Her case taught me that tuberculosis can masquerade as simply failure to thrive – nothing else.

I was constantly amazed at how many children with failure to thrive responded when I shot from the hip and administered anti-tuberculosis medicine.

Attempts to vaccinate against tuberculosis in Haiti have been fruitless. In the United States, tuberculosis was the leading cause of death at the turn of the twentieth century, but its incidence has gradually declined. Surprisingly, the anti-tuberculosis medicines invented in the 1940's had little effect on the declining rate. The improvement of economic status, along with the concomitant changes in housing and sanitation, was the main factor. Tuberculosis still persists in the inner-city ghetto population and will remain as long as the ghetto remains.

The Haitians were also bothered by minor but extremely irritating afflictions they contracted because of their close living quarters and frequent body contact. The worst of these was scabies. I could empathize with my patients since I contracted it four times.

Once called the seven-year itch, scabies could not have been invented even by the most imaginative sadist. When it first attacked I found myself occasionally scratching my wrists, a small nuisance. My scratching then spread it up my arms, to my armpits, then my legs and eventually my entire body. Showering made the itch worse, and when it was full-blown uninterrupted sleep became impossible. I woke up in the middle of the night violently scratching everywhere.

Scabies is caused by a hideous mite with four pairs of legs and massive pincer-like jaws that it uses to burrow into the skin. The diagnosis can be made by scraping a suspected skin lesion and finding this miniature monster under the microscope. In medical school, my dermatology professor told me that allowing the skeptical patient to view this creature encouraged compliance with treatment. This mite when situated then lays eggs, the reason scabies persists indefinitely when untreated.

Unlike the poor Haitians, I had the solace of knowing I would be cured with treatment. Every day at the clinics, I saw many patients with "gratel", "itchiness," who had hideous cases of scabies. They had huge scratch marks along their armpits and on their arms. The mite invaded the skin between their fingers where they clawed themselves in a futile attempt to obtain relief. The scratches bled and the unfortunates who had had scabies for years had tell-tale scars. Some scratches developed secondary bacterial infections requiring the addition of antibiotic treatment.

Scabies is cured with a lotion called Kwell, but the relief is not immediate. The itchiness is not caused by the mite itself, but rather by the allergic reaction to it; therefore a dead mite is just as annoying as a live one. While the lotion kills the mite, a month of constant skin turnover is needed to eject its corpse. All clothes and bedsheets must be washed to prevent reinfection. The poor Haitians lacked the necessary sanitary facilities and I doubt if I cured many cases. At least 80% of the Haitians had scabies and it was especially disheartening to see the starving children also being tortured by these little beasts.

The redeeming quality about scabies is that it was not lethal, unlike another disease I frequently encountered – typhoid. Along with malaria and yellow fever, typhoid helped Haiti win its independence when it ravaged the invading French army at the turn of the nineteenth century. It continues to ravage the Haitians.

Michelle was a young woman brought from one of the clinics to Sans Fil. She was lying in a bed with a high fever when I met her. Michelle was not a complainer and would have refused our hospitality had she not been penniless and unable to walk. She had a severe headache, abdominal pain, and diarrhea. Her exam showed little more than diffuse abdominal tenderness and anemia. I considered typhoid along with tuberculosis, malaria or a viral diarrhea.

The fever never defervesced. This confirmed typhoid, as both malaria and tuberculosis have intermittent fevers. To the astute physician, this reasoning represents poor judgement at best and gross incompetence at worst, as there are hordes of other problems that have an identical presentation. For example, appendicitis has a similar appearance; but since I did not have the necessary surgical equipment, there was little sense in considering this possibility.

I treated her with the antibiotic chloramphenicol. Typhoid is caused by a bacterium that calls the human digestive system its home. There it invades the intestinal mucosa, causing diarrhea. With each bowel movement it is excreted, and in Haiti it finds its way into the food and water supply, where it reinfects others.

Later in the day, a Haitian woman began screaming for me to examine Michelle. I walked over and saw an overflowing bedpan full of fresh blood where Michelle had just defecated. Michelle had just perforated a blood vessel in her intestine – the most feared complication of typhoid. She had verified my shaky diagnosis in the worst possible way. Quickly, I found a bottle of normal saline and placed an intravenous line in her arm. The saline poured in, but the blood continued to ooze out of her rectum. I had no blood to give her. Michelle appeared nonchalant as she faded out. The terrified look that I had become accustomed to seeing daily never crossed her face. Perhaps she welcomed death. Her last earthly view was that of a frustrated blan doctor helplessly peering at a bottle of saline.

The typhoid bacillus was not the only inhabitant in the Haitians' intestines; they also had worms. Although they rarely caused fatalities, these creatures infested the vast majority of the Haitians and literally sapped them of their blood and energy.

There were different species of worms and I had learned to identify them by the appearance of their eggs in stool specimens. It was a skill I soon forgot, since I only had one deworming medicine available and saw little sense in performing an academic exercise that did not change therapy.

One of the more common worms was the hookworm. The immature forms, or larvae, enter the human body by burrowing through the soles of the feet of a shoeless patient, causing an annoying itch. They are transported to the lungs via the bloodstream and lymphatics, resulting in a cough as they crawl up the windpipe. They are then swallowed and enter the intestines, finding a permanent home upon anchoring to the mucosa with their four sharp teeth. They feast on blood, rendering the poor patient anemic. Upon reaching adulthood, they lay thousands of eggs that are excreted in the feces. The eggs hatch in the soil and infect another shoeless patient, completing the cycle.

Another common worm was Ascaris, but unlike hookworm it is spread by directly ingesting its eggs that are found in the soil. Many of the children had "geophagy," which means eating dirt, a child's natural response to intractable hunger. As the Haitian proverb goes:

> Machwè brannen; grangou tchoule.
> Chewing anything helps to chase away hunger.

These eggs also contaminated the water supply and were even found in breast milk. Ascaris does not feed on blood, but skims the food its congenial host is digesting. They can grow to be a foot in length and can block the intestines, a surgical emergency. These worms migrate through the body causing abscesses and pneumonia.

Like flies, worms did not bother the Haitians as much as they did me. The mothers routinely saw worms when they changed their infants' diapers. They had folk remedies to eliminate them, but were not upset when unsuccessful. Rarely did a patient come to me complaining, "M'gen vè", " I have worms." To the Haitians, having worms was simply part of life.

Both hookworms and Ascaris were easily treated by giving a drug called Piperazine. Every child who entered the Children's Home was dewormed, and a child excreting a worm one-third its length was a common sight. Occasionally, a child would pull a worm out of his mouth. The sisters seemed to take a sadistic delight in showing them to squeamish visitors.

Another common disease, malaria, was caused by a smaller but more dangerous parasite. The name means " bad air" in Italian as early Italian physicians speculated that it is spread through this medium. They were close. The parasite is injected into the bloodstream by the Anopheles mosquito, a large insect that hovers like a bomb-laden airplane, circling until finding some poor person to bite. Usually I refuse to take medicine, but these mosquitoes intimidated me into complying religiously with the prophylactic anti-malarials.

When a human is bitten by an infected Anopheles mosquito, the immature form of the malaria parasite enters the blood and is absorbed by the liver cells. There they rapidly reproduce, bursting through the cell wall into the bloodstream, whereupon they enter the red blood cells to feed upon hemoglobin, the protein that carries oxygen. They again reproduce, and when they break out of the red blood cells the patient spikes a fever. These new parasites then find more red blood cells, restarting the cycle. The human host responds by making antibodies which, in their quest for the parasite, destroy the red blood cells, causing a severe anemia. Haitians, like blacks in general, have a high natural resistance to malaria because the disease has existed in Africa for eons. The development of sickle cell anemia is an evolutionary attempt to avoid malaria, and those with sickle cell anemia have less severe symptoms when they contract malaria.

Jean was a typical malaria patient. He presented during the peak of the rainy season, when the mosquitoes were breeding rapidly, along with ten others that day with the same symptoms. He had "lafiev e maltet", "fever and headache." He accurately described how the fevers came, first with a wicked chill that made his teeth chatter, followed by a profuse sweat that left him exhausted but relieved. He felt fine for several days until the fever returned. Jean did not need me to diagnosis his problem. He knew he had malaria and just wanted me to give him the medicine, Chloroquine.

I had a conservative approach when giving this drug. In many Third-World countries, especially in Southeast Asia, Chloroquine has been dispensed like water. The result was predictable; the malaria parasite evolved resistance to the drug. Now in these countries treating malaria is much more complicated and requires giving several drugs together, subjecting the patients to dangerous side effects. Fortunately, Chloroquine-resistant malaria has yet to be reported in Haiti and I was doing my part to maintain the status quo.

All malaria suspects had their blood examined to make a positive diagnosis. A drop of blood was smeared on a slide to dry. This slide was stained with a solution that lyzed the red blood cells while keeping the parasite intact. If the patient had malaria, I found colorful red purple signet-shaped parasites under the microscope. Sometimes I had to look for five minutes, but if I did not see the parasite, I did not give the Chloroquine unless the patient was severely ill.

Whites who had foolishly stopped their weekly prophylactic Chloroquine also contracted malaria and found their way to my care. Since they do not have the same natural resistance, their symptoms were more severe than the Haitians and some were close to death. Everyone improved, but I did not have malpractice insurance, so I avoided treating Americans. It is truly a sad state of affairs when the first thing one thinks of when looking at a sick patient is one's liability.

Malaria is a pleasure to treat because the patients improve quickly. By being given five white pills, a febrile exhausted human being was transformed into a happy energetic individual in a matter of days. Few diseases have such dramatic results with simple treatment.

The key to success was patient education. I spent hours instructing my patients on how to take the medicine and then having them repeat the directions until I was satisfied they understood. Since the vast majority were illiterate, I would take a piece of paper and draw a picture of the sun rising, the sun high in the sky, the sun setting and the moon in the sky. Each picture represented a time of day. Then I would draw a sketch of the pill under the appropriate scene so that the patient knew when to take the medicine. Malaria patients often became nauseated, and regurgitated their medicine. One of the good sisters almost died because she could not keep Chloroquine in her stomach long enough to be absorbed. I had to administer her medicine intravenously before she began to recover.

Not all patients with malaria had typical symptoms. Gerrette, an 8-year-old girl admitted to the Children's Home with severe malnutrition, was one of these inconsiderate individuals. She had no fevers, headaches or abdominal pain, but each day she became more visibly anemic – her dark skin turning to café-au-lait. Because she had no appetite, her body became too weak to mount a fever. Her only request was that she not be harassed by compulsive blan doctors. Her blood was replete with parasites, including the mature forms that indicate a chronic case. With chloroquine, she improved so quickly that I thought it was Voodoo. The sisters sent her to school since her family could not afford it. Because of her case, I screened every child admitted to the Children's Home for malaria.

While malaria typically caused fever and anemia, a chronic infection sometimes resulted in kidney failure. The sisters brought a young man to Sans Fil. He had a bloated face, distended abdomen and swollen legs. A microscopic examination of his urine showed "hemoglobin casts," columns of coalesced red blood cells, indicating kidney destruction. His blood was full of malaria parasites. With chloroquine, he slowly lost the excess water as his kidneys began to function. His balloon-like face developed eyelids and cheeks, returning to its normal appearance.

The worst complication was when malaria entered the brain. Doing battle with cerebral malaria was a fight I rarely won. While I was rounding one Sunday, a missionary priest arrived with an anemic comatose muscular young man who was dying. The priest told me he was walking and talking the previous day but had complained of fevers and severe headache. He had "changing mental status," an indication for an immediate spinal tap to rule out meningitis. Day deftly performed the procedure and when he pulled out the stylet, the spinal fluid gushed out rather than dripping slowly as usual, indicating increased pressure. His blood was full of malaria parasites, but the spinal fluid was clear. This meant that the malaria had inflamed his brain, causing the spinal fluid pressure to increase.

There went the afternoon. Actually my health was spared by caring for this patient. The only time I did not work was Sunday afternoon, when I "relaxed" by playing softball with the Marines who guarded the American Embassy. Being a card-carrying weekend warrior, I found that these games inevitably resulted in my injury, either from spraining my ankle tripping over first base or displacing my front tooth after plowing into a Marine twice my size while chasing a fly ball. In all my stay in Haiti, I never got seriously ill, although I treated the worst diseases on the planet; however, I barely survived these violent softball games.

This gentleman, whose name I never learned, died in spite of my best efforts. His coma was so deep that he would not respond to the most noxious stimulus I knew—a ringing tuning fork on the nose. My only success with cerebral malaria was a woman who came to me —still conscious—who described perfectly having brain-crushing headaches and high fevers. She also had a high pressure when Nick did the spinal tap and her blood was full of parasites. Not only did I give her steroids and Chloroquine, but as she was nice enough to come on a weekday, I could get blood from the Red Cross in downtown Port-au-Prince.

The Red Cross is truly a wonderful organization, well-deserving of its Nobel Peace Prize. I was a regular there, and although I transfused scores of patients, no one ever had a transfusion reaction. Even with their limited equipment, their technique was flawless and they bent over backwards to obtain any blood type I requested.

My patient with the cerebral malaria did not respond initially and after several days of treatment, death was imminent. But then her headache abated, and soon after she developed the most important sign, an appetite. Within two weeks, she was helping to clean and feed the other patients and then left, going back to her world. This patient did well, not only because of the treatment but because of early diagnosis. Comatose patients with cerebral malaria always died.

Like everything else I treated, the solution to malaria was not having doctors dispensing pills. The vector that spreads it, the Anopheles mosquito, has to be destroyed. In a more idealistic era, this seemed to be possible. The breeding grounds were sprayed with the pesticide DDT and the swamps were to be drained. It just did not work. The mosquitoes developed resistance to DDT and political factors made swamp drainage impossible. Perhaps the goal was unrealistic. Indigenous malaria existed in the United States until the 1950's, and to transfer this effort to areas that have not developed representative government is not to be feasible in just a few decades.

Malaria, like typhoid, tuberculosis, hepatitis, diarrhea and the other afflictions I dealt with every day will not be eradicated soon. Haiti must achieve the economic development that would permit it to afford the necessary plumbing, vaccines, nutrition and swamp drainage. One thing I learned in Haiti is that these diseases certainly will not be eliminated by doctors.

Chapter 6

Pills Don't Help if the Patient Doesn't Eat

Grangou nan vant pa dous.
Being hungry is not sweet.

Haitian proverb

Most of the diseases I treated stemmed from malnutrition. Although I knew malnutrition was devastating, I never realized how this condition could permeate all aspects of life until I lived in Haiti.

The malnourished Haitians had no energy. The few jobs available to them required the demanding manual labor of a pre-industrialized society: pulling trolleys full of heavy bags of charcoal, carrying water over miles of mountainous terrain, or plowing a field without a tractor or animal. This type of work requires a tremendous amount of energy; thus lumberjacks eat more than accountants. No amount of will power can make a body that ingests a biscuit and sucks on sugar cane perform a decent day's work. The problem was compounded by Haiti's oppressive heat. I myself found it impossible to put in a good eighteen-hour day, a feat I performed easily as an intern in an air-conditioned hospital in the United States. Yet many outsiders construed the Haitians as being lazy. Nothing could be further from the truth.

Malnutrition also robbed Haitians of their intelligence. Starving pregnant women deprived their unborn children of the proper nourishment for neurological development; thus these children were born mentally impaired and their continued starvation during the crucial months of infancy exacerbated their underdevelopment. During infancy, the brain grows rapidly, which is why children have a proportionally larger heads than adults, an anatomical detail neglected by the Renaissance artists. For every bout of severe malnutrition, a child loses ten intelligence quotient (IQ) points. Some visitors I met while in Haiti had adopted starving children from Third-World countries. Although they loved them, they all noted one thing – these children did poorly in school.

The immune system functions poorly in the malnourished, not only rendering the Haitians more susceptible to disease, but also lengthening their recovery period. Frequently I sutured the wounds of men who engaged in machete fights over women. Often the wounds reopened because poor nutrition impaired the healing process. When I sutured the face of an American friend who cut his face during one of our barbaric softball games, it healed in a matter of days.

The fear of hunger changes the human psyche completely. Haitians sold the medicine I gave them to purchase food. They saw little sense in taking medicine while starving to death. When the choice was between food versus medicine, food won.

After what I saw, I was embarrassed that my country pays farmers not to grow food and purchases surpluses to maintain food price stability – while 500 miles from our shores human beings starve to death. However, I was to learn that starvation in Haiti is a complex problem that is not easily rectified.

There are many types of malnutrition, varying from specific vitamin deficiencies to total calorie deprivation. Like most American-trained physicians, I was abysmally ignorant of nutrition, since it is not stressed in medical school curriculums. While some see this as a nefarious plot by the American Medical Association, physicians in the United States rarely see primary malnutrition unless they are working in a deprived area. Malnutrition secondary to cancer and alcoholism is common, but can not be treated without attacking the underlying problem. Also, hospitals have trained dieticians who spend their time trying to convince potbellied armchair athletes not to drink a six-pack of beer every day or telling diabetics that they would not need so much insulin if they did not eat two bowls of ice cream after dinner. Consequently, American physicians rarely deal with nutritional problems directly unless they are attempting to tap the lucrative diet market.

In Haiti I quickly learned the gamut of the varieties of malnutrition along with their proper treatment, because most patients had one form or another.

Edith was typical of the type called "marasmus." Although nine months old, she weighed only eight pounds, slightly above the average weight of an American newborn. Her hairless head was triangular with a large indentation caused by the slowly closing fontanelle, indicating both dehydration and retarded bone growth. Her ears were downturned and her black eyes sunk deep in her skull. When she grimaced, showing her toothless mouth, the skin folds of her forehead radiated circumferentially above her eyebrows, giving her the appearance of an wizened 80-year-old woman. Too weak to cry, she looked at me wondering what crime she had committed to deserve being born.

When I picked her up, she deposited green diarrhea on the two-dollar sandals I had purchased at the famous Iron Market in downtown Port-au-Prince. Her tiny hands groped over her body, scratching the rampant scabies that infested the sores around her armpits, legs and groin. Her ribs were clearly demarcated, bulging through her translucent brown skin and converging on the breastbone which pointed into her ballooned abdomen – a phenomenon seen in starvation because of excess intestinal gas production. The vertebrae protruded from her back and her entire scapulae were visible, not just the winged portions or shoulder blades. Instead of buttocks, she had only sagging skin folds that hung over her thighs. Completely lethargic, she was not upset as I poked and prodded her emaciated stick-like frame, finding an enlarged liver, overworked because it was metabolizing the little protein that remained in her muscles to provide life-sustaining energy.

Marasmus is the type of starvation caused by total calorie deprivation, the type whose heartrending photos are used by charity organizations to solicit contributions. Her mother told me the same story I heard ad nauseam all year. The father was dead, a euphemistic way of saying he had abandoned them. She had four other children, no house, and no money. Furthermore, although she was trying to breast-feed Edith, she had little milk.

A woman requires 600 extra calories a day to manufacture enough milk for her child. Breast milk provides enough calories until a child is six months of age. Even in Haiti, infants appeared healthy until breast milk was inadequate and the mother could not afford to supplement their diet.

Poor Edith was starving. Her mother was too malnourished to maintain her own body, let alone manufacture breast milk for another. Even if Edith improved, she would still be smaller than her well-nourished age-matched peers. Rarely did I see a tall lower-class Haitian. They still existed in the Dark Ages and never achieved the growth spurts seen in the well-nourished baby-boomers of the industrialized world. This improved nutrition produced athletes who smashed records considered unbreakable – such as women who swam faster than Johnny Weismuller. On the other hand, there are already many tall upper-class Haitians and Haitian-Americans who are becoming athletic stars.

After a protracted battle, Edith improved. I was impatient and tried to feed her with high caloric food. Her diarrhea persisted. In spite of me, she eventually became a healthy roly-poly child, and when I worked in the clinics I would see her in the food lines with her mother, hopelessly dependent on us, but at least alive.

Children with marasmus did well if they had no other serious illnesses. All they needed was food. On the other hand, there was another type of malnutrition that had a higher mortality rate – "kwashiorkor." Named after the Ghanian word for "deprived child," kwashiorkor affects children who have adequate caloric intake, but lack protein. Protein holds water in the bloodstream, so that a low level results in fluid leakage and total body swelling.

Human beings, unlike most animals, lack the biochemical ability to manufacture protein from other foodstuffs such as carbohydrates and fats; therefore, it must be in the diet. The problem is that protein-containing foods such as milk, eggs and meat are too expensive for Haitian peasants. This, coupled with ignorance about nutrition, resulted in a large number of babies with kwashiorkor.

Kwashiorkor was usually accompanied by marasmus. Some reseachers are of the opinion that attributing this condition to low protein is an oversimplification and that kwashiorkor represents a failure of the body cells to control their borders, allowing water to cross them. Whatever the cause, the consequences were always tragic.

The kwashiorkor children had a uniformly eerie appearance. Their entire body was swollen, so that to the uninitiated physician, the diagnosis appeared to be renal failure. They peered between edematous eyelids, aware of, but uninterested, in their surroundings. The corners of their cracked lips oozed a fluid that looked like strawberry Kool-Aid, not the deep cherry red of normal blood. Their bodies were covered with circular flat ulcers that blended with their pale brown skin. There was no scar tissue or pus. These children were so sick that their bodies could not even mount an inflammatory response. Their abdomens bulged with ascites, causing the umbilicus to protrude, and their hands swelled like inflated rubber gloves – spherical orbs with five protuberances. The legs ballooned, and in the girls the swelling extended up to the labia and buttocks, where the skin eroded, exposing the red raw underlying dermis. In the boys both the scrotum and penis swelled. The mothers ignorantly retracted the overlying foreskin, bunching it up like a rubber band; this caused the tip of the penis to swell enormously and crack. It was a good argument for mandatory circumcision.

The most striking feature of the kwashiorkor babies was their unnatural red hair. By stretching it, I could see stripes of black – the band sign. These black bands indicated periods when the child received adequate protein, whereas the red hair reflected a time of protein scarcity. It was like looking at the rings of a tree.

> Lamizè fè chini manje tabak.
> Poverty makes the caterpillar eat tobacco.

These hapless children were completely apathetic. I would prod their abdomens, look in their ears, open their mouths – invading their bodies without inciting a retaliatory effort. They were like Play-Doh; I could set them up to listen to their lungs and then lay them down to feel their abdomen. Only when I punctured their foot to check for malaria would I get a slight objection – a feeble kick, a weak swat, or a brief groan. This was the state of thousands upon thousands of children in Haiti.

Joseph was a typical child with kwashiorkor. With the characteristic total body edema, translucent brown skin, red-orange hair and a scrotum the size of a baseball, he looked like an Oriental with mumps. His shins had a thick black eruption caused by a niacin deficiency. He wore a New York Yankee T-shirt – his worse prognostic sign, as they had just clutched defeat from the jaws of victory, losing their chance at the play-offs. Joseph and I would play for considerably higher stakes.

For the next three weeks, Joseph and I did battle – he tried to die while the good sisters and I struggled to keep him alive. My first step was to start an antibiotic, although I could not find the etiology of his fever. His lungs were clear, but I suspected he had a pneumonia; however, since his debilitated body could not muster an inflammatory response, no abnormal lung sounds emanated from his chest. Malnutrition is rarely alone.

Joseph refused to eat, listlessly lying in bed preferring to be left alone. The sisters tried to force cereal in him, but he just vomited it. I had no choice but to put a tube down his nose and into his stomach – a nasogastric tube. Thus I could drip milk into his stomach at a slow constant rate so that he would not vomit and – I hoped – not develop diarrhea from malabsorbtion.

Initially Joseph would not respond, but I had learned that the key to treating malnutrition was patience. Patients require the same amount of time to recover from an illness as they did to develop that illness. Since Joseph did not develop into this state overnight, he would not recover overnight.

Two days later he was still febrile, so I added another antibiotic ending his fevers, perhaps serendipitously. He refused to eat, but was tolerating the milk given to him through the nasogastric tube. As his edema disappeared, his eyes widened, the skin on his feet shriveled and his face shrunk.

Then it happened – the dreaded diarrhea began. He was no longer tolerating the most dilute milk possible, but stopping it was out of the question. It was the only source of nutrition. Running out of options, I decided to give him a blood transfusion, as his hemoglobin level was only five, one-third the normal level. This was not without risk, as his malnourished heart pumped inefficiently and might not tolerate the large fluid load.

After obtaining blood from the Red Cross, I assembled the necessary apparatus for starting an intravenous line. Although Joseph looked moribund, some primordial instinct enabled him to fight like a wolverine when the needle punctured his skin. Writhing and kicking while the sisters held him, he made placing the intravenous line a challenge, but this was the first sign of life he exhibited. Fortunately, I found a good vein in his arm and within seconds the intravenous line was in place. Ritualistically, I taped the needle to his arm and began the transfusion. Everything went smoothly for five minutes, then the blood stopped flowing. With a syringe of saline I flushed the tubing. Joseph screamed in pain as the saline formed a small welt in his arm. The intravenous line had infiltrated.

Grudgingly I found another vein, and after five minutes of eternal agony for both of us, the blood was again flowing smoothly. Five minutes later, it stopped. My reaction the last time was mild annoyance; this time it was outrage. He had no good veins left in his arms and it was 7:00 PM. I had been working for the past ten hours in this oppressive climate; I was exhausted, hungry, and thirsty; but this child was dying, had a hemoglobin of five, and needed the blood.

When stressed, my mind blames anyone but myself. It was Joseph's fault the intravenous line came out. I had placed it perfectly and he moved. I was impervious to the fact that I may have taped it poorly or used the wrong needle. While learning to place intravenous lines in medical school, I silently cursed obese patients whose veins were difficult to find. As I was trying for the third time – the poor patient in pain while I probed under his skin with a needle – I could not help but think, "It's not my fault you eat too much. If you would control yourself, I would not be having such a difficulty." Upon finishing, I felt guilty and apologized for the discomfort I had caused. The patients were always more forgiving than they should have been.

I now shaved half of Joseph's scalp and inserted the intravenous line in his head. Five minutes later, the blood stopped. I was beyond anger and to the point of despair. I wished I could have gotten the intravenous line and stuck it in my own arm. But I did not need the blood – Joseph did. I concluded that the needles I was using were too small and found one with a larger bore, knowing that it would be more difficult to insert. This became apparent when I blew the last vein on his shaved scalp, causing a huge hematoma that bled for ten minutes, even though I pressed on it tightly while poor Joseph whimpered and cried.

Joseph had endured four needle sticks, and now I proceeded to shave the other side of his head. The bottom line was that he needed the blood. Again with a large bore needle, I penetrated the skin resulting in an outcry and several strong kicks. Slowly, I angled the needle towards a bulging vein, moving cautiously, waiting for the quick flash of strawberry Kool-Aid that told me I hit paydirt.

Bang! I got it.

Again I started the blood. It flowed slowly, but with the larger bore needle, it never stopped. After two hours of torture, Joseph was finally receiving his blood. I felt quite stupid for not putting in a large bore needle the first time and saving us both from this ordeal. It reminded me of a Haitian proverb:

> Sòt pa touye ou, men li fè ou swe.
> Being stupid won't kill you but it will make you sweat a lot.

I would like to say that the next day this life-giving blood had improved him; that he sat up in bed, ate spontaneously, laughed and wanted to go see a Kung Fu movie, but Joseph looked as miserable as ever, his only activity being to pull out his nasogastric tube.

"M' ap mange, m' ap mange", "I will eat, I will eat", he pleaded. I was not impressed. I jammed the tube into his nose and pushed it into his stomach.

Over the next several days, though, Joseph's energy increased slightly. He started to sit up in bed and even had a mild interest in a storybook I showed him, teaching me the Creole words for some of the pictures. His fingernails and conjunctiva became pinker and his hemoglobin increased to eight. He started to eat some of the cereal the sisters made, but still required the nasogastric feedings for most of his nutrition. Then he began to ambulate, slowly pacing while holding on to something and solemnly staring at me, wondering what torture I had in store for him. I think he improved out of fear of what I would do to him if he did not.

With all his edema gone, Joseph now looked like a child with marasmus. I stopped his antibiotics, so he now was receiving only food and vitamins. He even began to take some interest in his environment, playing with the other children and coloring.

Then it happened—the voracious appetite appeared. No morsel of food was safe. He ate only one meal a day—all day. When he was given a bowl of rice, he devoured it in five minutes and then individually picked out the remaining kernels until not a single one remained. He was never without a piece of bread in his hand. As Nick would say, I was "over the moon" when I finally pulled out his nasogastric tube.

In one week, he gained five pounds. He smiled mischieviously as he tore through the Children's Home, being a general nuisance and interfering with the sisters' work. He even forgave me for all the torture he had suffered at my hands and asked me to take him outside. I took him to a nearby store, showing him to the proprietor and explaining the hard work it took to get him healthy. The proprietor thanked me for helping Haiti. Nonetheless, this did not stop him from trying to overcharge me for a soda.

I was always amazed at the enormous quantities of food children like Joseph could eat. Sometimes it would take four weeks until their appetite developed; but when it happened, there was no question. Nothing was more satisfying to see. These children were on a search and destroy mission, their eyes rapidly scanning everywhere, seeking something they could gobble up.

In early life humans require a large food intake. An infant needs 40 calories per pound a day, whereas an adult needs only 10. A child Joseph's age requires 20; however, a recuperating malnourished child makes up for lost time tripling its food requirement and eating 60 calories per pound a day! To ingest this awesome quantity of food requires munching on something every waking hour.

Joseph was a triumph, but there were also failures. One of my first was a two-year old child brought to the Children's Home with severe kwashiorkor. However, when I examined him the inside of his mouth was dry and his heart rate was 150 beats per minute. When he cried no tears welled up in his eyes. Although he was edematous, he was also severely dehydrated.

I quickly placed an intravenous line in his scalp, but knew enough to rehydrate him slowly, since he was so malnourished. Nonetheless, with the additional fluid he swelled up even more, to the point where his eyes were swollen shut and the skin covering his feet cracked. I was forced to decrease the fluid rate to the point it was barely physiologically significant.

I did not know what to do; I was between a rock and a hard place. His vascular system was not functioning. All the fluid I poured into his bloodstream immediately leaked out to the extravascular spaces where it was useless because it was unavailable to transport nutrients and red blood cells throughout the body. The child was literally dying of thirst in a sea of fluid.

I wished I had the backup of an American hospital, with expert nurses, crackerjack pediatricians, sophisticated laboratory tests and expensive protein intravenous solutions. At least the child may have had a fighting chance. In the next hour, he deteriorated rapidly, his respiratory pattern becoming sporadic and his eyes deviating in opposite directions. The sisters informed me this means impending death. They were right.

It was a problem I saw many times – children with both kwashiorkor and dehydration. Very rarely did they live. I would ask the mothers why they had waited so long before bringing the child to us. They always had the same answer, telling me they had taken the child to the Hôpital Général, where they had received a prescription for vitamins and protein supplements. These cost more money than the mother made in two months. By the time they came to us, it was too late.

Babies with kwashiorkor would seem to be improving, then deteriorate suddenly. One child came to the Children's Home almost dead. She was only three-months old, and her mother, who was wearing a T-shirt portraying Jean-Claude and Michèle Duvalier, was so malnourished that she produced no breast milk. The child was whiter than most Caucasians, reflecting a hemoglobin of three. She was wearing a knitted blue and white cap and her cadaverous face was swollen, with pale pink lips and puffy eyelids that were almost transparent. She had a ragged green pullover dress that contrasted with her bright red diapers, stained with bloody diarrhea. She was bleeding from her intestines.

I put in a nasogastric tube for feeding and transfused her. I felt that her death was imminent but, to my surprise, after several days she developed a small but significant appetite. The next day, while I was rounding, one of the sisters noticed that she was not moving. I walked over to investigate and discovered why. She was dead.

While I was laboring in my mind about what could have gone wrong, Dr. Eustauche, a Haitian pediatrician who occasionally stopped by to help me, dropped in. A woman of 40, she was one of the upper-class Haitians who volunteered her services. She told me that Haiti needed a Indira Gandhi to start a massive sterilization program.

I did not even greet her – I was so upset – and immediately asked her opinion. She had treated many patients with kwashiorkor and told me that they "crashed" like this all the time. She suggested a myriad of possibilities – low body temperature because the child was close to the window, feeding too fast, too much protein and fluid from the blood transfusion, low sugar etc.

Incidents like this taught me how to treat kwashiorkor. The best teacher in medicine is experience and I was learning by trial and error, mostly error. In this case, the patient may have died no matter what I did, but with her improved appetite I felt she had had a fighting chance that evaded me.

I read numerous books and articles on the management of malnutrition. Although they were replete with conflicting opinions, they all agreed on one thing – the key to success was a specific diet that gradually replaced fats, proteins, vitamins and minerals. If they were administered too rapidly, the body would reject them. In a way, it was similar to transfusing blood. If a patient has a slowly bleeding stomach ulcer that decreases the hemoglobin to eight, replacing this blood in a matter of hours is foolish. Over the past several months, this patient's body has compensated for the decreased hemoglobin and will rebel, perhaps by going into heart or liver failure.

The same reasoning applied to children with kwashiorkor; they were not ready for steak. The excess protein would cause them to lose their fluid too rapidly, rendering them dehydrated, or else the protein would not be absorbed, resulting in diarrhea. Patience was key. I had to begin with a small amount of protein in their diet and increase it if they tolerated it.

The first step in caring for a malnourished child was to determine its weight. This enabled me to estimate the amount of food to give. If the child had an appetite, it was fed "labouyi," a dilute protein mixture that resembled cereal. It was easily absorbed, so it rarely caused diarrhea. Children without appetites had to be fed milk through a nasogastric tube, an art that took me several months to master.

I made the formula from the available ingredients: powdered milk, simple sugars and vitamin supplements. In spite of their African background, most of the infants tolerated this, but in those who developed diarrhea, I had to switch to the lactose-free milk – when it was available.

Each child had a daily protein requirement, the main constituent of the powdered milk. This was not enough to supply the necessary calories, so the deficit was compensated by the addition of simple sugars. Then I added vitamins and water and stirred. The solution was suspended in a sterile container and dripped slowly into the child's stomach via a nasogastric tube.

The main problem was that the milk was viscous and would not drip through at the low rates. Hanging the container from the ceiling still resulted in insufficient pressure. I enlarged the bore of the tubing – no luck. One day while in a particularly clever mood, I placed the milk in a plastic bag and squeezed it with a blood pressure cuff. The milk splattered all over the room. Then I tried increasing the rate of the solution and giving it over a shorter length of time. This had the predictable result – the children decorated the floor with their vomitus. I was driving the poor sisters crazy.

At this point I imported the only high-tech American contraption I ever used in Haiti, the IMED. IMED's are electronically powered intravenous solution pumping machines and are used in intensive care units to titrate exact amount of fluid necessary in critically ill patients. Several telephone calls to an altruistic physician from Wisconsin brought several to Haiti.

Other than needing a degree in astrophysics to operate them, the IMED's functioned beautifully. They even had battery reserve so they still worked when the government turned off the power. I could now feed a listless child without hovering over him constantly.

Soon my experience and reading allowed me to develop a protocol for treating malnourished children. Everyone was started on antibiotics, vitamins and deworming medicine. Basing my calculations on the weight and appetite, I individually tailored each child's diet and adjusted it daily, depending upon whether weight was being lost or gained. Those with pure marasmus should gain weight immediately while those with kwashiorkor needed to lose weight gradually. These children had to diurese their excess fluid initially but not rapidly enough that they became dehydrated. Treating them was a precarious balancing act.

I learned whom I could save and whom I could not. Babies who were comatose, premature or had massively enlarged livers died in spite of my best efforts. Perhaps someone smarter than I could have done better. Nonetheless, there were many patients I did not treat because I felt my time was better spent on others.

Most of the malnourished children also had specific vitamin deficiencies. Vitamins are substances that are vital for the body's biochemical reactions, but do not provide energy – like carbohydrates – or serve as building units – like proteins. The vitamin requirements of human beings are minimal – much to the chagrin of the charlatans who push vitamin tablets down the throat of the American public – and are easily fulfilled by eating three balanced meals a day. This is why one bowl of cereal can provide the minimum daily vitamin requirement. In Haiti, though, where eating three meals a day is a fantasy, a variety of vitamin deficiencies occurred. While they were usually combined, I sometimes saw these deficiencies in their pure forms.

The most tragic of these was vitamin A deficiency because it sometimes resulted in permanent blindness. Jean, a 3-year-old with kwashiorkor, was saddled with this problem. I diagnosed it from across the room because his corneas, the clear part of the eyes that covers the irises, were opacified. The whites of his eyes had also lost their luster, and were a muddy wrinkled brown.

"Li wè?", "Does he see?" I asked his mother.

"Wi," she replied.

A quick flash of my hand in Jean's face proved her to be incorrect. Jean did not flinch. The mother was denying the problem.

Vitamin A, or carotene, is responsible for maintaining a clear cornea. This is why carrots, which have a high concentration of carotene (thus the name), are touted to improve vision. Vitamin A contributes to the eye's ability to see in decreased illumination; thus the the first symptom of Vitamin A deficiency is night blindness. Young children are rarely able to verbalize this complaint, but when an adult Haitian complained of poor night vision I immediately started him on Vitamin A.

I treated Jean with high doses of Vitamin A but to no avail. He needed a corneal transplant, although it is doubtful the graft would have taken, given the severity of his disease, his malnourished state and the inability of his mother to follow the complex postoperative instructions in the unsanitary environment of Cité Simone.

Fortunately, most cases of Vitamin A deficiency were not as progressed as Jean's and caused only mild corneal irregularities. Many malnourished children teetered on the brink of Vitamin A deficiency, depending on what food was in season. Mangos have large amounts of Vitamin A and the incidence of this deficiency decreased notably when they were available. The Children's Home often had several patients with dull corneas that returned to complete transparency with high doses of Vitamin A.

Another seasonal disease was pellagra, which is caused by a lack of niacin, one of the B vitamins. A young girl I saw during clinic had a classic case. Her mother told me she had "feblès e dyare" or "weakness and diarrhea." Although she was emaciated and lethargic, the child's most striking feature was a black thick rash rising above her brown skin on her shins, arms and face. It formed a deep black necklace around her neck. She smiled sheepishly as I asked her to open her mouth revealing a raw, painful, beefy red tongue.

Niacin is instrumental in cell formation; therefore, body tissues with rapid cell turnover such as the tongue, skin and intestinal mucosa are affected. Thus a sore tongue, skin rash and diarrhea are among the typical symptoms.

Medical students remember pellagra with the mnemonic, the 4 D's – dermitis, diarrhea, dementia and death. Fortunately, this child only had two of them. She was taken to the Children's Home where I gave her a daily injection of high dose B vitamins along with other supplements. A key point in treating vitamin deficiencies is to give all the vitamins since giving only one precipitates other vitamin deficiencies. After a month, the rash was almost gone and she left, fifteen pounds heavier.

I saw pellagra constantly among both adults and children. One-third of the clinic patients had shiny skin, swollen feet and a black crusty rash on the shins and arms. Although niacin is found in many foods, these people could only afford to suck on sugar cane. Many did poorly even with treatment, because they had so many other problems too.

One unexpected problem was Vitamin C deficiency or scurvy. In the nineteenth century an English physician noticed that sailors developed impaired blood-clotting ability while at sea. He traced this problem to a lack of citrus fruits – which contain Vitamin C – in their diets and recommended they be fed limes. To this day, English sailors are still called "limeys." As Haiti is replete with citrus fruit – oranges, grapefruits and limes – and they are fairly cheap, I got the impression that scurvy was due to ignorance as well as poverty.

The first child I saw with scurvy looked at me pensively, as if I were the first white face he had ever seen. Then he began to cry, opening his mouth and revealing huge, bleeding, friable gums. On his legs were black-and-blue welts – hematomas – caused by bleeding under his skin. Vitamin C is crucial in the repair of damaged blood vessels, so that in scurvy a small bruise that should stop bleeding, continues to ooze, forming hematomas. In the United States, this child would be assumed to have either leukemia or hemophilia.

I asked the mother, "Kisa ou ba li pou manje?", "What do you feed the child?"

She replied, "pen e sik", "bread and sugar."

I questioned further discovering that she had no money to buy milk or meat and she rarely gave him citrus fruits.

I told her that the child needed fruit for proper nutrition. She nodded politely, probably just to humor the crazy blan doctor who was blathering about the wonders of a balanced diet when she was barely managing to keep the child alive.

I found some Vitamin C elixir, poured it into a cup and gave it to the child. He spit it out even though it was sweet. I saw no sense in arguing – the tube went down the nose followed by large doses of Vitamin C. Miraculously, the hematomas resorbed and the gums stopped bleeding after a week. I reiterated the need to the mother to feed him "chadèk" – a fruit resembling a grapefruit – which was still in season.

The sisters, like many missionary organizations in Haiti, tried to address malnutrition by distributing food. Everyday at Sans Fil, I saw hundreds of people standing in line waiting for their allotment. Most waited patiently, although there were occasional incidents when someone would try to skip line, causing a ruckus that was quickly quelled by a huge intimidating man the sisters had hired to keep order. As I walked by most smiled politely, but some stretched out their hands, asking for money.

They stood in the oppressive heat – shoeless old men with ragged pants and shredded shirts clutching assorted buckets, bottles and bags; women breast-feeding their infants while their other children clung to their colorful dresses while sucking their thumbs – their mainstay of oral gratification.

Many were handicapped from polio and had makeshift canes to support themselves. They all moved slowly, even when it was their turn to receive food. They had nothing – no energy, no money, no work, no security, no place to sleep – nothing. They were professionals and standing in this line was their job. They were hopelessly dependent on the miniscule handouts of the industrialized world. Sometimes I would sit down and watch them.

One man, after receiving his portion, sat on the ground eating rice and beans from an oatmeal can with his hands. He had on a yellow-plaid shirt, baggy gray pants and a red baseball cap that said "International Harvester." He had one leg, so he carried a crutch which came in handy as he used it to defend himself from a boy who attempted to steal his food. His one remaining eye continued to scan while he ate, searching for others who dared to harass him.

Another woman reverently approached the statue of the Blessed Mother that presides over Sans Fil, stretched out both her arms and began mumbling some prayers. She had two crutches wrapped with rags under her armpits since she was missing a foot. A white and blue polka-dot handkerchief encircled her head, exposing only her earlobes, from which large white round earings dangled. Attired in an ill-fitting azure dress that descended to mid-shin, she had a wide plastic pink belt tied around her waist, as she was too skinny to use the buckle. Around her neck were two crucifixes, one wooden and the other metal, that hung between the cups of her padded bra. After finishing with her requests, she got in line.

The sisters distributed whatever they had available – rice, wheat, beans, corn, milk or bread. Their biggest supplier was Andrew Simone, who sent food all over the world – Africa, South America, the Caribbean and Asia. Because of him, thousands of people survive who would otherwise die of starvation.

Andrew had a soft spot in his heart for Haiti and visited frequently. He spoke with bitter emotion about world hunger. He realized that the problems were political, but was convinced, perhaps correctly, that there is enough food-making capacity to feed the world five times over. There was no excuse in his mind for the present worldwide starvation.

What Andrew does is buy food surpluses from the Canadian government with his own money. He, his family and his friends then personally load massive containers with the food, place them on ships and send them all over the world. Andrew explained to me why he was able to do this.

Canada, like the United States, assures itself of a steady food supply by promising farmers that it will purchase their crops that can not be sold. This results in excess food that the government must buy and then figure out what to do with it. Often, it ends up in storage and rots. Andrew purchases this food at a very cheap price and gives the government the assurance that he will not place it on the international market, where it will depress prices.

This is why it is possible to sponsor a foster child in a Third-World country for only twenty dollars a month. The food already exists so the money just has to pay for the food's transportation. Ostensibly, this helps everyone, the government has political stability because there is enough food, the farmers make a profit and the poor in the Third World get fed.

I had another friend who was an economist from Holland. Between his futile attempts to beat me at chess, he presented a less rosy scenario. Eric's job was to advise developmental organizations in Haiti on how to maximize food production. He also helped these organizations bring food into Haiti so that they could feed the starving. He told me that this did not require any economic wizardry, just knowing who to bribe.

Eric was committed to feeding the starving in Haiti but like most who do this work for a protracted time period, he was hopelessly cynical. People like Eric delighted in teaching naive idealists like me how the world works.

Like Andrew, I too was bitter when I saw the massive hunger and asked Eric why the governments of the industrialized world could not simply donate food surpluses to Third-World countries. Eric just laughed, telling me that most Third-World governments could not care less if their people starved. These governments would not distribute food to their starving but would instead sell it on the international market, using the profits so that their elite could purchase condos in Manhattan. This would cause the industrialized nations to compete with the food they had just donated for free.

Eric continued, telling me that his work is damaging Haiti in the long run. The organization that employed him was bringing food into the country and distributing it to the starving for next to nothing. This forces the peasant to compete with free food. Eric pointed out that, unlike in the industrialized world, most laborers in Third-World countries make their livelihood in agriculture. Free food destroys their economy. The poor peasant pulls his plants out of the ground and stands in line and waits for his allotment. Eric told me that the United States routinely destroyed local economies with free food when it opened its arms after a natural disaster, like a flood in India or and earthquake in Mexico. He compared it to another country giving away free cars in the United States. It would demolish the already-weak automobile industry.

I asked Eric why more work was not being done to make Haiti produce its own food. He told me there already were many programs in Haiti to increase the productivity of the Haitian peasant. Agricultural groups brought tractors to increase food production, but the peasants, superstitious and bewildered, had no idea how to maintain such machines. When they inevitably broke, they attributed it to God's will. Foreigners who tried to repair them met with continual frustration. Since the phones rarely worked, there was no way to call for spare parts. One had to travel to an urban area and battle with listless operators to contact someone overseas to send them. Then came the challenging task of getting them out of customs. This entailed goading self-serving bureaucrats to find them and required bribes, not to mention a huge tax. By the time the parts arrived, the tractor had rusted and could not be repaired.

More important, Eric said, the peasants have no interest in making their land more productive. The common conception is that the Haitians are lazy; however, the real reason is that they seldom prosper from the fruit of their labor. Productive land is confiscated by local politicians. A peasant's title to his land is vague, and since he is illiterate, he does not know what it says. When his land is stolen, he has no recourse.

The more I worked in Haiti, the more I realized Eric was right. One time, some group donated kosher pickles. The sisters distributed this novel item and what followed was amazing. Within hours, they were for sale everywhere in Port-au-Prince. As I rode home on my moped, smiling vendors walked up to me at the red lights offering the pickles at a bargain price – two dollars. Fortunately, Haiti did not have an indigenous kosher pickle industry that could be destroyed.

Some of the people who received free food at Sans Fil immediately went to the nearby outdoor market to sell it. I heard them bargaining with the vendors, trying to get the best price possible. The women sitting there buying the food are not stupid. They knew it is distributed for free. When they return to the countryside to replenish their supplies, they will be able to bargain for a lower price. The poor peasant who produces it can not compete with free food.

From dawn until dusk, I wrestled with malnutrition. Although I never acquiesced to its existence, I came to the sober realization of why it is so difficult to redress. The more I thought about it, the more depressed I became so after a while, I just stopped thinking about it and did my best to treat the individual patient in front of me – whether it be a child with kwashiorkor, an infant with scurvy, or an adult with marasmus. This was all I could do.

Chapter 7

Creating a Nation of Pariahs: The AIDS Fiasco

AIDS, SIDA, it didn't start here.

Lyrics from popular Haitian song

When I first told people I was going to Haiti, those who did not confuse it with Tahiti reflexively commented, "Don't catch AIDS."

No other issue, not even the American occupation of Haiti after World War I, could cause a Haitian's blood to boil as did this topic. Bringing up AIDS in the company of Haitians is a faux pas I committed only once. After seeing firsthand patients with AIDS, hearing about the discrimination Haitians suffered because of it, and witnessing the devastation it inflicted on Haiti's already weak economy, I understood the reason.

AIDS, or Acquired Immune Deficiency Syndrome, is a failure of the body's immune system to fight off infections. With every breath and with each scratch, human beings are constantly bombarded by hordes of viruses, bacteria, protozoa and fungi. The immune system battles to destroy these invaders, but AIDS victims are defenseless, so that routine infections become killers. To date, no one with AIDS has survived more than ten years.

In the late 1970's, scattered reports surfaced about patients with rare and inexplicable infections; but, it was not until 1982 that a study from the Center of Disease Control in Atlanta characterized the symptoms of AIDS and found that the affected patients fell into at least one of four categories – homosexuals, intravenous drug abusers, hemophiliacs and Haitians. Further research revealed that this disease is associated with a virus named HIV-III and that the transfer of this virus is required before an individual can acquire AIDS. Millions now harbor this virus, but the percentage who will acquire AIDS is uncertain. Presently it is estimated to be between 30 and 40%, but this percentage has been found to be higher for those who have harbored the virus for several years, leading to speculation that everyone with the AIDS virus could contract AIDS.

Apparently for individuals to acquire the AIDS virus, it must enter their circulatory system. Thus homosexuals transmit the virus if their blood mixes or when the semen of one sexual partner contacts the blood of the other, a frequent occurrence in anal intercourse, since rectal tissue tears easily. On the other hand, intravenous drug abusers spread the virus by sharing needles, thus mixing their blood.

Hemophiliacs are congenitally deficient in a crucial factor for blood clotting and require transfusions to prevent themselves from bleeding to death. This factor must be pooled from the blood of hundreds of donors, so that if a single one has the AIDS virus, the hemophiliac can contract it. Screening procedures have cleared the blood supply in the United States although theoretical contamination is possible since the test only detects the antibody to the virus, not the virus itself. This test was unavailable in Haiti and the fear of giving contaminated blood tempered my enthusiasm for transfusing patients.

Why AIDS has appeared in Haitians is a subject of intense debate. Unlike with the other three groups, no specific behavior or medical need explained the incidence of AIDS in Haitians. To this day, the scientific community has not succeeded in explaining the rationale for this association; however, they did inadvertently succeed in unleashing a wave of discrimination and bigotry that continues to stigmatize the Haitians to this day.

When AIDS was initially reported, only about 5% of its victims were Haitian. Black-Americans, Hispanics and whites all comprised larger groups; however the vast majority of them were either gay, hemophiliac or used intravenous drugs. Rather than investigate the Haitian connection further, researchers singled out being Haitian as a risk factor based on ethnic association only.

The problem was that the physicians writing the initial studies were English-speaking Americans who knew nothing about Haitians or Haitian culture. They asked "Do you use intravenous drugs?", "Are you homosexual?" and got "No" for an answer. Some of the more clever researchers asked the same questions in French and got the same answers. These shoddy methods prompted Dr. Ary Bordes, the Haitian Minister of Health, to comment that the studies "had quite a few flaws."

When Haitian AIDS victims were interviewed by other Haitians in their native Creole, it was discovered that many of them did indeed fall into the other risk groups. Poor Haitians speak no English and little French, although they often claim otherwise, and did not understand the questions initially posed. Secondly, homosexuality, although practiced in Haiti as it is in all societies, is a big taboo and gay Haitians would not admit to it, even under intense questioning by native speakers. Also, some of these AIDS victims turned out to be homosexual prostitutes but did not consider themselves to be homosexual. They were just trying to support themselves and their families the only way they could in a country with 50% unemployment.

But none of this mattered. After the media-generated hysteria, AIDS and Haiti became synonymous in the minds of Americans. This destroyed their tourist industry, discouraged business investment, justified the unfair detention of Haitian immigrants, subjected Haitians visiting the United States to a multitiude of embarrassing questions and innuendos, and caused Haitian-Americans to suffer housing and employment discrimination.

Business investment had been increasing in Haiti in spite of the political climate. The industrious Haitian laborer produces everything from computer cables to baseballs at one of the lowest minimum wages in the world, less than $3.00 a day. But when American retailers refused clothing labled "Made in Haiti," potential investors were scared. Furthermore, the managers who were needed to start a business refused to live in Haiti.

Tourism had been diminishing since the mid-seventies, but the AIDS fiasco was its death knell. In the winter of 1981-1982, 70,000 tourists came to Haiti. The following winter, there were 10,000. As in most Caribbean islands, tourism is crucial to Haiti in maintaining foreign exchange reserves, especially the powerful American dollar. This dramatic decrease cost Haiti 25,000 jobs, and most of them were lost by poor people who worked as maids, waiters, cooks, vendors and translators. Many hotels closed and those that remained open eked out their existence with 25% occupancy. While living in Haiti, I was able to rent a hotel room for less than $5 a day.

To blame Haiti's poor tourism entirely on the AIDS hysteria though, is an oversimplification. Haiti does not have a strong middle class to hold down prices, so lodging and food are expensive. Tourists who speak neither Creole nor French get the impression they are being cheated, an impression that is not entirely incorrect. Car rentals are colossally expensive and the traffic jams in Port-au-Prince that occur when the traffic lights turn off because of a power shortage would perplex even a Roman. One can sit in an intersection for forty-five minutes in 105 degree heat. There is only one golf course and it is just nine holes. Most tourists I met in Haiti were in the process of changing their itinerary.

Cruise ships once came daily but the passengers refused to disembark, knowing that they would be inundated with dozens of beggars pushing starving babies in their faces. This is the last thing relaxing vacationers want to see. Avoiding aggressive vendors is impossible. Even when one is swimming at the beaches, vendors paddle their boats beside tourists, holding up chains and necklaces. One tourist told me that when she left Haiti, she was going to look out her airplane window to make sure there was not a Haitian in a parachute trying to sell her something. The government put messages on television requesting that tourists not be harassed, but the vendors I saw did not appear to be in any position to purchase televisions.

But the AIDS stigma made this poor industry worse. Previously there were few tourists, now there were virtually none. This was especially evident when I shopped for souvenirs. Before leaving Haiti, I had to buy a wedding present for some friends so I went down to my favorite shopping spot, the Mache Fè, or Iron Market, in central Port-au-Prince.

The Mache Fè is a huge, roofed enclosure surrounded by a red wrought-iron fence. As I approached, I caught the attention of the outside vendors. The women stood up in their long colorful dresses and straw hats holding up cards, watches, chains, sandals and assorted trinkets. A well-built young man wearing a button-down shirt, gold chains and sunglasses thrust a stack of 100-gourde notes in front of my face. I asked him the rate.

"Five percent for one hundred dollars American." he responded in slightly accented English.

I was not interested but told him that he could never hold that much money out in New York.

"This is not New York," he said smiling.

There were many black markets in Haiti, but these gentlemen always gave me the best rates if I had cash. They had a large cash reserve from laundering the money the drug dealers made selling marijuana and cocaine to Haiti's upper class.

I pushed my way inside and immediately become the cynosure, the "blan" who wanted to buy something. There were at least one-hundred booths selling everything – statues, masks, oil-paintings, pastels, etchings, clothing, tableware – some of it junk, but most of it good quality work made by the cheap but industrious Haitian work force. I looked around and to my disbelief, not only was I the only white, I was the only customer! Here in the largest, best-stocked tourist market in all of Haiti I was alone – courtesy of the AIDS hysteria.

I was soon surrounded by a sea of smiling black faces, jostling for position to get my attention. They all looked like recent graduates of the Dale Carnegie school of salesmanship.

One woman shouted, "I have prices most cheap for you."

I asked her if she had tableware but she did not understand so I translated my question into Creole. She only sold statues. I could see the dejected looks of the others when they heard my Creole. They now knew they could not overcharge me.

Suddenly a tall man burst through the crowd, extended his hand, and introduced himself as "Mr. Chip." Dressed in a gray suit coat and matching fedora, he beckoned me to examine his paintings while peering at me through his two-tone sunglasses. I did not buy any, but I at least taught him how to say "Mr. Cheap."

By this time several people had offered to be my guide. I needed one so that I could shop uninterrupted, but I could not find my old buddy from previous visits. Then he appeared; his limp quickened and a big smile crossed his face as he spotted me. He could not tell me his name, as he was mute, and I suspected he had been crippled from birth trauma or meningitis. Nobody bothered me when I was with him, since the hawkers knew he had some influence over which merchants I patronized. A nod of his head told me whether I was paying a fair price for something. After I left, he would return to the merchants that I bought from, for a cut of the action.

After wandering around for several minutes, I found a booth with tableware and became interested in a hand-carved mahogany salad bowl complete with six serving bowls and utensils. It would be hard to find for less than $100 in the United States. Trying not to appear too interested, I inquired as to the price.

The proprietor, another apparent Dale Carnegie graduate, grinned from under his straw hat.

"Fifty dollars."

In Haiti bargaining power is directly proportional to one's fluency in Creole, so I switched.

"Sa se pi chè", "That's a bit high."

Unintimidated, he told me labor costs were going up.

We politely bickered, the price gradually coming down. Being a veteran of many market battles, I knew the two key elements to successful bargaining. The first was to avoid offering a counter price until the last minute. Otherwise, the price was fixed at the average of your offer and his previous offer. The other was to never give the vendor the impression that you were doing him a favor by patronizing him. Haitians are proud people, and if insulted will refuse to sell.

We settled on eighteen dollars, much less than it was worth but probably more than a Haitian would pay for it. I could have paid ten dollars if I had wanted to, but being the only customer in the store gave me an unfair advantage, especially since I came from the country that propagated the AIDS hysteria. I did not even ask him for a "degi" "bonus," a common Haitian bargaining technique.

AIDS was used as an excuse to violate the rights of illegal immigrants who came to the United States. While the American government granted legal status to 100,000 Cubans, 8,000 Haitians remained in legal limbo. Many were retained without due process under the guise of being disease vectors.

Even Haitian-Americans were not safe. Some who had jobs were fired abruptly, especially those who were illegal aliens. They had no legal recourse. Parents were afraid to send their children to school with Haitians. Haitians trying to sell their houses had to accept half their value. Others were thrown out of their apartments without even having their security deposits refunded. Unlike homosexuals, who could hide their orientation when economically necessary, blacks who speak English with a Creole accent could not disguise themselves.

One Haitian businessman told me that when he went to the United States the customs agent would open his passport with a special pair of tweezers he reserved for Haitians so that he could protect himself from AIDS. The indignities were endless.

The Duvalier government reacted in characteristic fashion, arresting known homosexuals, jailing male prostitutes and closing hotels in the Carrefour district that were known as homosexual hang-outs. Although these homosexuals were given "reeducation programs," this did not revive the tourist industry.

At the Hôpital Général, the AIDS patients were sequestered in a bleak windowless room where they became non-persons. The sisters obtained permission to feed and clean them since no one else would do it. Occasionally, nurses were seen. With their starched immaculate white uniforms, neatly bunned hair and impeccable posture, they appeared to be the epitome of professionalism. The slightest suggestion that they care for an AIDS patient caused them to roll their eyes upward, as if to say, "You expect me to touch that?" As more AIDS victims arrived, they overflowed into the Depot and then eventually arrived at Sans Fil, where I cared for them.

Diagnosing AIDS with absolute certainty was difficult since I lacked the laboratory facilities to identify its characteristic organisms or subclassify white blood cells, a test that documented a poorly functioning immune system. However, there were many patients who had the clinical picture of AIDS – fevers, interminable diarrhea, weight loss, generalized lymph node swelling, and persistent cough. Miliary tuberculosis and other conditions may appear similar, but when these symptoms were accompanied by a history of sexual promiscuity and fungal infections, the diagnosis was obvious.

André had a classic case of AIDS. Stricken with weight loss, a chronic cough and continuous diarrhea, he was emaciated but did not have the disheveled appearance of my other patients. His skin was smooth and glistening, surprisingly free of the erosions of scabies, but instead he had white translucent nodules over his chest and arms, miniature warts. He had the bull neck of a linebacker – which looked out of place on his stick-like frame – caused by grossly enlarged lymph nodes. His mouth was full of white blotches, "Candidiasis," a fungal infection seen in immune-compromised patients. I listened to his lungs, hearing a pneumonia in each lobe.

"Ou homosexuel?", I asked.

He did not respond, and thinking he may not have understood me, I switched to another expression.

"Ou masisi?", "Are you gay?"

Again he did not respond, but the other patients in the room began to snicker. Seeing that I was compromising his privacy, I stopped this line of questioning, as it was not going to change my treatment but merely satisfy my curiosity.

I continued my examination, looking in his rectal area.

The skin around his anus was eroded, exposing a wet pink undercoating that was surrounded by amorphous yellow-brown excrescences, Herpes warts. Andre was a homosexual prostitute.

Taking my ophthalmoscope, I looked into the back of André's eyes. This is one of the most spectacular views in medicine, allowing a view of the retina, the brain's extension to the eye. Normally, one sees a pinkish-white circular optic nerve surrounded by an orange-green sea, with smooth slender arteries and veins coursing through it. But Andre's retina looked like a battlefield, with blood from ruptured blood vessels scattered amidst white streaks of infarcted nerve tissue, the so-called "ketchup and cottage cheese" retina. Andre had a viral infection of his retina "cytomegalovirus," which was diagnostic of AIDS. Looking into the eyes was a good way for me to diagnosis AIDS.

"Ou wè byen?", "Do you see well?" I asked.

"Pa pi mal" , "All right."

This did not surprise me as I saw no blood in the macula of either eye, the area of the retina most responsible for clear vision.

My job was to keep Andre comfortable. Since he had a fever of 104 degrees and was dehydrated, I walked away to find some Tylenol and the equipment for starting an intravenous line.

"Li gen SIDA? Li gen SIDA?", "Does he have AIDS? Does he have AIDS?", the other patients asked.

The power of an American-media blitz is awesome. Even the poorest of the poor knew about AIDS.

"No," I lied. I was not about to see André run out of Sans Fil like the lepers.

However, they must have suspected my transgression as they watched me glove my hands before starting the intravenous line, something I had never done before. I placed it without difficulty but took great care not to stick myself with the needle. I was not afraid of catching AIDS in Haiti, but took care not to let the blood of a potential AIDS victim touch me.

Nobody bothered André and he lived for three weeks comfortable and pain free until he quietly passed away in his sleep. In a sense, André was lucky to be in Haiti. In the United States, he would have been subject to a variety of tortures of which even the most imaginative fire-and-brimstone preacher could not conceive. Even a member of the Moral Majority, who concluded AIDS was God's revenge for wayward behavior, would wince when he saw what AIDS victims endured during attempts to cure them.

In the United States André would have had multiple spinal taps, skin biopsies, lung biopsies, brain biopsies, eye biopsies, tubes up his rectum, tubes down his throat, tubes down his nose, tubes in his penis, needles in his arteries, needles in his veins, needles in his eyes and spears in his bones. He would have taken drugs that made him vomit bile, lose his hair, made him dizzy, burnt his skin and destroyed his kidneys. He would have had CAT scans, liver scans, kidney scans and bone scans. He would have been inundated with internists, proctologists, oncologists, ophthalmologists, hematologists, neurologists, dermatologists, pulmonologists and nephrologists, all ordering different tests to justify their consultation. After being harassed by residents, tortured by interns and bored by social workers, he would still have died. André was much better off in Haiti.

AIDS was not confined only to men in Haiti, women prostitutes contracted it also. One patient I cared for told me she made a decent living in the nearby red light district, Carrefour, catering to the "blan bet", "the stupid white." Unlike most prostitutes I had cared for, she was candid about the details of her livelihood. I asked her if the cards that the prostitutes carried certifying they were disease free were valid, since visiting Americans who fraternized with the natives often asked me this question. She laughed, telling me that no one was even examined, all the prostitutes did was pay money to obtain the card. This confirmed my suspicion that these American businessmen gave their wives other gifts besides Haitian artwork when they returned.

I told her my method of discouraging the advances of Haitian prostitutes. When I first arrived I would tell these aggressive women that I do not have any money, but they persisted, knowing that a blan had money by definition. Then I tried telling them I was studying to be a priest, but this just made them laugh, making me wonder how seriously Haitian priests took their vow of celibacy. Finally I arrived at the ideal response; I told them I was gay. My patient thought this was clever and agreed with me that this statement would discourage all but the most aggressive prostitutes.

She had lost weight rapidly in the past three months and complained of "feblès." I examined her, noting enlarged lymph nodes everywhere and a fungal infection in her mouth. Another doctor was visiting, so I asked his opinion. While we discussed her case, I watched her eyes move adroitly from mouth to mouth, the way mine did when I was struggling to understand a foreign tongue. She knew that we thought she had AIDS, but never asked me directly. She dwindled away for a month, until only a skeleton with a blood pressure so low that it seemed incompatible with life, remained. Finally, she died.

It was cases like hers that confounded the experts. Although a prostitute, she did not fit into the initial high risk groups – homosexual, intravenous drug abuser or hemophiliac. Perhaps as a prostitute she had had anal intercourse with an infected customer. But what became apparent from her case and others like it was quite disconcerting: AIDS is also spread by heterosexual transmission.

The AIDS virus initially was only found in blood and semen but further research revealed its presence in other body fluids – saliva, tears, urine, vaginal and cervical secretions. This opened up new avenues of possible spread – avenues that public health officials previously thought did not exist. In 1982 a New York woman, who had no other risk factors, contacted AIDS from a bisexual man. In Boston, a man who had an affair with the wife of a bisexual husband died of AIDS. As more cases of heterosexual transfer of AIDS appeared, it was noted that most of the patients were sexually promiscuous – either prostitutes or individuals who had had at least 50 sexual partners in a 5-year period. With this mounting evidence, the Center of Disease Control decided to list heterosexual contact as a risk factor in 1984.

When the Haitians with AIDS who did not fall into the initial risk groups were reexamined, many, but not all, were found to be either prostitutes or promiscuous. Other factors not operative in the United States also surfaced. Like most poor countries, Haiti had many cases of neglected venereal disease, a fact I was reminded of every clinic day when I saw sex organs with open raw sores. This could have facilitated the transfer of the AIDS virus just as the open rectal sores enabled it to be transferred in homosexuals. Also, epidemics spread more rapidly through sick malnourished populations. Unfortunately, the initial researchers who targeted Haitians as a risk group did not know this and classified being Haitian in itself as a predisposing factor for AIDS.

The question still remains, though, "How did AIDS get to Haiti?". The answer changes practically on a daily basis, prompting New York Times medical reporter Dr. Lawrence Altman to label the enigma as a "jigsaw puzzle without a picture." The political stakes are almost as high as the medical ones, with the civil rights of the gay community and the fragile economies of Third-World countries hanging in the balance.

In 1977 the first known case of AIDS appeared in Paris in a Portuguese taxi driver who for several years had had rare intractable fungal and protozoal infections. After bewildering numerous physicians, he was discovered to have a poorly functioning immune system, and eventually he succumbed. When AIDS was later described, he was diagnosed retrospectively to have had it. He and many other early cases found in Europe had one thing in common – they had been to Central Africa.

Many scientists are convinced that the AIDS epidemic began in rural Central Africa either by a mutation of a virus or as a previously unknown disease that existed, but did not spread until unemployed farmers began to migrate to the cities. Here, in the urban environment of prostitution and promiscuity, the epidemic spread.

There is some evidence to support this theory. Frozen blood serum samples from as early as 1973 have been found to have the AIDS virus and now an estimated 10,000,000 Central Africans harbor the virus. Diseases associated with AIDS, such as Kaposi's sarcoma, a rare form of skin cancer, had been commonly diagnosed in Central Africa for previously unknown reasons. As homosexuality is uncommon, it is thought to have spread heterosexually by unsterilized needles used to give vaccinations or by blood-sucking mosquitoes. Nonetheless it was not until the early 1980's that wealthy Africans, who go to Paris and Brussels for their health care, began to present with AIDS. African health officials have bitterly fought the notion that AIDS began in their countries pointing out that it could have started as mutation in the Western world's gay community and was then brought to Africa by tourists. An editorial in the *Ghanaian Times* summarized theories establishing Central Africa as the origin of AIDS as "this shameful, vulgar, foolish attempt by white supremacists to push the latest white man's burden to the doors of the black man." African physicians pointed out that the first cases were seen in the industrialized world, not Africa.

The enigma is further complicated by African Swine Flu, a disease of pigs that has the same symptoms in pigs as AIDS does in humans. These infected pigs are found in two places, Central Africa and Haiti. It has been theorized that the disease is transferred by blood-sucking ticks from pigs to humans, but to this date a common virus has yet to be found. Whether there is a link or whether this is a red herring remains to be seen.

There are many ways AIDS could have spread throughout the world. European and American workers and tourists may have carried it back to their respective countries. When the colonial powers of Portugal and Belgium ended their domination of parts of Central Africa in the early 1970's, Russia filled the vacuum and required Cuban troops to do so. Some of these potentially infected soldiers arrived on the shores of the United States during the marialito boat lift which occurred in the late 1970's.

One way or another, AIDS ended up in the gay bathhouses of New York City and San Francisco, where an unprecedented sexual revolution was taking place. While homosexuality has always existed, for the first time in modern history homosexuals had access to random unfettered anonymous sex. The drug amyl nitrate enabled gays to maintain erections for hours, longer than the most macho undrugged male, allowing dozens of sexual partners in a single evening. "Fisting" in which a fist is thrust up the rectum of a sexual partner, ripped and tore the fragile rectal mucosa. Further anal intercourse caused the blood and semen to mix frequently.

The promiscuity of the gay community allowed it to spread, so that now about 70% of urban gays harbor the AIDS virus. The first gay AIDS victims averaged 1200 sexual partners a year. Even before AIDS was discovered, numerous diseases were proliferating in the gay community that were usually seen in the Third World, such as the protozoal diarrheas of amebiasis and giardia. This prompted one physician to compare Manhattan to a tropical island. Thus the HIV-III virus spread exponentially throughout the gay community, and in several years millions were infected with the AIDS virus, tens of thousands had AIDS, and thousands had died—the disease having tragically killed young men in the most productive years of their lives.

There is no paucity of theories to explain why AIDS was found in Haiti. It has been speculated that bizarre Voodoo rites involving the drinking of pigs' blood allowed the African Swine Flu to enter humans. AIDS then spread by closet homosexuality, blood-sucking mosquitoes and inoculation with unsterile needles. Perhaps this mysterious disease was brought from Central Africa by Haitians working there in the 1960's and early 1970's. The frequent travelling of Haitians between New York and Port-au-Prince furnished another possible conduit.

But to the Haitians all these theories were nonsense. The source of AIDS in their country was obvious—American tourists. Their feelings were best summarized by Dr. Ary Bordes who said that Haitians were "victims, not carriers" of AIDS. American tourists had come to their country, enjoying a veritable sexual buffet among impoverished people who will do anything for $5, and spread AIDS. The American scientific community was using Haiti as a scapegoat rather than imply irresponsibility by the politically powerful gays. Who better to blame for AIDS than a poor black nation whose populace did not even speak English? They were hiding the fact that AIDS had been spread heterosexually in Haiti because of the hysteria this information could unleash in the United States. AIDS was all over the Caribbean, but other islands suppressed these data to protect their tourist industries, the bulwarks of their economies. If this is true, AIDS epidemics could eventually appear all over the world giving new meaning to the expression "Yankee imperialism." The Haitians felt they had been screwed, both literally and figuratively. While in Haiti I was forced to listen quietly while Haitian doctors I met harangued about the unfairness of this stigma. They were especially outraged by the medical arrogance of American doctors who implied that they could not make proper diagnoses in their own people. Haiti did its part and allowed American physicians access to Haitian patients, and in response to their hospitality they were stigmatized.

There is evidence to suggest that AIDS was indeed brought to Haiti by outsiders, possibly American tourists. Prior to 1980, there are no known cases of AIDS in Haiti and a review of pathological specimens at the Hôpital Gènèral substantiated this premise. Haitians were noted to have a high incidence of AIDS only because recent immigrants converged upon the hospitals of New York, Miami and

Newark. AIDS turned up in Dominica, Tobago, Martinique and Jamaica, indicating a diaspora of the AIDS virus. Unlike Haiti, though, these countries did not have as large a recent immigrant presence in the United States.

Furthermore, no visitors to Haiti contracted AIDS before 1980. The French, who are not known as having strong commitment to celibacy, had vacationed in Haiti with immunological impunity. Also of note is that the initial cases of AIDS were concentrated in the Carrefour district, a known hangout for gay American tourists. AIDS was virtually non-existent in rural Haiti until the late 1980's.

Hemophiliacs did not contract AIDS until the early 1980's. This is significant, because up until 1976 much of the cryoprecipitate (a concentration of the factor deficient in hemophiliacs) was from Haiti, since the pharmaceutical companies took advantage of the willingness of Haitians to sell their blood at a low price.

Jean-Jacques Dessalines and Toussaint L'Ouverture would have applauded in their graves if they knew how the Haitian scientific and political community launched a powerful assault against being stigmatized with AIDS. All warring political factions united and lobbied extensively to have themselves removed as a risk group. One letter to the *New York Times* by a Haitian physician noted that the incidence of AIDS was higher in New Yorkers than Haitians. He asked, "Why weren't New Yorkers singled out as a high risk group?".

The struggle culminated in this unprecedented letter published in medicine's most prestigious journal, *The New England Journal of Medicine.*

> The Republic of Haiti has suffered a severe injustice over the past year in the American press. Countless broadcast and print journalists have related stories attributing the origins of the acquired immunodeficiency syndrome (AIDS) to Haitians, without sufficient factual data to support this theory. Recently, press reports have reflected a shift in opinion about the origins of the disease. Unfortunately the new evidence often has been hidden on the inner pages, while damaging information about the alleged Haiti-AIDS connection has appeared in front page stories of American newspapers and journals.

Haiti already is the victim of a negative image in the United States, exacerbated by the tendency of the media to ignore coverage of positive steps taken in Haiti toward liberalization and democratization. The volume of media stories relating Haitians and AIDS cast a pall of gloom over the country, deterring potential business investors and tourists from venturing too near. The negative impact on our already distraught economy has been tremendous.

It is puzzling to contemplate the reasons for selecting Haiti as a target for origination of the dreaded AIDS problem. We sympathize with all AIDS sufferers and hope a cure will be found before hundreds more fall prey to this deadly menace. Haiti, however, has sufficient problems without being selected as a scapegoat for a mysterious ailment that has, sadly, descended largely upon the American homosexual community.

We as a black nation, well understand the pains of world discrimination and trust that a free, democratic system like the United States' would be particularly careful to ensure that its medical conclusions are based on objective, thoroughly researched conclusions and not on biased conjecture.

The time is well overdue for the record to be set straight regarding AIDS and the Haiti connection. I am sure responsible institutions like yours will uphold your admirable American tradition of unveiling the truth.

Fritz N. Cinéas
Ambassador, The Republic of Haiti
September, 1983

The movement was partially successful. In 1983 the New York Health Commissioner removed Haitians as a risk factor for AIDS, and in 1985 the Center for Disease Control followed suit. However, Haitians are prohibited from donating blood.

The origin of AIDS in Haiti may never be known. What is apparent now, though, is that the Haitians as an ethnic group do not have a higher predisposition to AIDS than anyone else, and today only

3% of AIDS victims are Haitian. When one considers heterosexual transfer along with the other risk factors, most if not all of these Haitian cases can be explained. Since Haiti does not have a large indigenous homosexual community, AIDS was spread heterosexually. Now AIDS is beginning to be seen more frequently in the United States because of heterosexual contact.

Unfortunately, the discrimination against Haitians persists, and Haiti's tourist industry has yet to rebound. To this day, when I tell people I worked as a doctor in Haiti, those who do not confuse it with Tahiti remark, "I hope you don't have AIDS."

Chapter 8

A Permanent Blackout

Riddle: A fly enters a room. Each day, the number of flies in the room doubles so that by the sixtieth day, the room is full of flies. When is the room half full?

Answer: The fifty-ninth day

Once again, I had a flat tire. I stopped at one of the many curb-side repair shops, which consisted of two young men with a tire iron and patching equipment, and had it repaired. It cost five gourdes and I knew it only cost five gourdes, but as usual, they were trying to gouge me for quadruple the price. The discussion was still in the polite stage when my repairman, a muscular adolescent, spotted an attractive girl walking by.

Without even excusing himself, he made a beeline for her. Unlike American men, he did not waste any time and immediately asked her if she wanted to have sex that evening, even pointing to a rendezvous point. His friend, in case I did not understand, got a silly smile on his face, and explained to me in sign language what they were discussing. He made a circle with his thumb and index finger, then licked the index finger of his other hand. He placed this wet finger in the "O" he had formed and moved it rapidly in and out.

After watching this display, I said to the girl – who already was aroused – "Ou pral vini ansent", "You will become pregnant."

She looked at me, tensed her lips and opened her almond eyes wider, puzzled.

"Ou pral vini ansent", I repeated.

She looked at her seducer, not upset that I was forcing my opinion on her, but bewildered by the strange statement this crazy blan was making in barely comprehensible Creole. She understood me, at least the words that I had said. But it did not take a mind reader to deduce that this information was news to her. She had no idea that there was a relationship between sexual intercourse and pregnancy. Actually, I should not have been surprised as many American ghetto teenagers do not know about the birds and the bees either.

I continued, telling her that she would not be able to feed the child but I may as well have been talking to my tire. She walked away, flashing a smile at her lover, neither comprehending nor caring about what I had said. The salivating repairman, who I think already had had a premature ejaculation, took my dollar with no further argument. He had more important topics on his mind. I imagined this girl standing at one of our clinics in the near future holding her emaciated and dehydrated infant.

Tens of thousands of babies that can not possibly be supported are produced annually in Haiti. Haiti, with 700 people per square mile, is already the most densely populated country in the Western Hemisphere. It is more than coincidence that it is also the poorest.

It was in the 1950's that generalized awareness of overpopulation began, with dire predictions of worldwide unemployment, famine, breakdown of social structures and war. While these predictions were not entirely accurate, the population bomb is still ticking, and in some Third-World countries such as Haiti it has already exploded.

In some circles, it has become fashionable to minimize the population explosion, as worldwide birth rates are declining faster than previously expected. Nonetheless, between 1950 and 1980, the population of the Third World doubled from 1.7 billion to 3.4 billion. Even with the most optimistic predictions it will have doubled again by 2030. Most of the decline in population rate has occurred in China, which is employing draconian measures, and in the industrialized world, thus skewing the statistics. Meanwhile, the population of Africa has doubled in the past 20 years. In the next 25 years it will double again. Tragically, it is not likely that food production and economic growth will keep pace. Disasters such as the mass starvation in Ethiopia may become commonplace.

Catholicism is Haiti's official state religion, although Protestant religions, especially fundamentalism, are rapidly making inroads. One missionary I met joked that Haiti was 80% Catholic, 30% Protestant and 90% Voodoo. I initially felt that the Catholic Church's prohibition on birth control is the main cause of the high birth rate, but after working in Haiti and learning to speak Creole I found this to be a gross oversimplification. The high birth rate is due to many complex factors that I saw firsthand every day—ignorance, poor family structure, increasing urbanization, the cultural role of women, the need for security in old age, the lack of economic development and the unavailability of birth control devices and methods. I later learned that the presence of industrialization is a much greater prognosticator of a country's birth rate than religion. Thus Ireland, which has not legalized abortion and has the Angelus on television daily, has a lower birth rate than non-industrialized Singapore, which not only has legalized abortion, but also offers economic incentives for uneducated women to remain barren.

Haiti's population grows at a rate of 2.2% a year as opposed to that of the United States, which grows at 0.7%. This figure is arrived at by taking the number of people who are born and subtracting it from the number of people who die or emigrate and converting this number to a percentage of the population. Actually, Haiti has a low population growth rate for a Third-World country because the death rate is so high. Nonetheless, the population of Haiti, like that of the rest of the Third World, will double by the year 2025, and unless there is drastic change there will not be a similar increase in economic growth.

When Haiti achieved its independence in 1804, the peasants went to the countryside and resumed their primitive African farming methods. This depleted Haiti's soil, so that the burgeoning population forced the peasants to cultivate mountainous land by stripping its trees to feed themselves. The wood is burned and sold as charcoal, Haiti's main source of energy. The results are predictable. With each rainfall, Haiti's precious topsoil flows into the ocean, and Haiti's eroded mountains are visible to anyone flying into the country during the daytime.

Reforestation attempts have been fruitless, their main accomplishment being to distribute bumper stickers that say "Ou menm, ou plante pyebwa in Ayiti?", "You, have you planted a tree in Haiti?" The government has even resorted to guarding the remaining forests, but the peasants simply encircle the trees with a single cut destroying the trees' circulation system, so that several months later they fall. It is difficult to induce behavior that is in Haiti's long-term best interest in people who are starving. If the present trend continues, Haiti will be treeless by the end of the century, a green paradise converted to a desert in a matter of generations, just as the once-thick forests of Ethiopia are now lifeless plains full of starving people.

Without trees, the water table decreases so that the reservoir that furnishes Haiti's only hydroelectric power plant is low, causing frequent blackouts. A home-based generator is standard equipment in the homes of the elite and business investment is discouraged by the lack of a reliable power source.

Unable to sustain themselves in the countryside, the peasants have been forced to emigrate to the cities, searching for non-existent jobs. The cities, without proper sanitation and housing, are unable to absorb this influx resulting in enormous slums and shantytowns. The population of Port-au-Prince has doubled in only ten years. The closed living quarters of such massive urbanization destroys the family structure exacerbating the population problem.

Especially discouraging was the pitiful women I cared for. Routinely I saw them; they were in their mid-thirties but looked fifty, with their sagging breasts and their frames battered by a dozen pregnancies. When they stood up, their wombs protruded out their vaginal opening and their rectums prolapsed out their anuses. Their multiple pregnancies had stretched the muscles that support these structures to the point where they were functionally useless. Of their 12 children, 4 were alive.

In Haiti a woman's role is to reproduce. It is her cultural imperative, elevates her social status and makes her desirable as a wife. As the Haitian proverb goes:

> Lè ou pa gen pitit, ou se chen.
> When you don't have children, you are a dog.

When a woman had a child, her social status increased meteorically. On the women's ward at Sans Fil I learned that there is a subtle complex hierarchy. Even if I lived in Haiti for forty years I would never understand it, but its most overt manifestation was the clothing the women wore. These loving, docile women would become tigresses, savagely fighting over the clothing sent as donations. Those high on the pecking order decked themselves out in colorful handkerchieves, bracelets and chains. Those who lost sobbed for hours simply because they did not get the belt they wanted. More than clothing was at stake; it was their status.

Visitors would come and distribute jewelry, often to the weaker and sicker patients. The pandemonium that erupted was unbelieveable. A lower status woman could not keep a nice piece of jewelry unless she had an Uzi. The other women ganged up on her, beating her and disrupting her few belongings until she gave up the desired status symbol.

It is similar to the corporate structure in the United States. As one rises up the ladder, one must follow strict guidelines – such as moving from a Chevrolet to an Oldsmobile to a Cadillac. Woe to the man who violates this unwritten code – who appears with a Gucci belt while his superiors have Pierre Cardin, or who dresses his wife in an ermine coat at the annual Christmas party while the boss's wife is attired in imitation mink. He will soon be doing flange inventories in northwestern Montana.

When one woman who was staying at Sans Fil had her baby, she was permitted to have a new wardrobe – a bright red dress, earrings, gold-colored bracelets and even a bra. There was no argument; she deserved it. She had fulfilled her role and reproduced. It did not seem to matter that she had no husband, no job, and no support. She was a mother, period.

In rural Haiti there exists a complicated family structure that extends beyond the nuclear family. Unfortunately, the increasing urbanization has caused this structure to disintegrate. One day at the clinics, within fifteen minutes I found three children with severe kwashiorkor who needed to go to the Children's Home. Each of the mothers were pregnant and they had had six, eight and ten children. None had husbands but they continued to generate babies. This is why at least one-fifth of the children die before they are five-years-old.*

One time I became so upset that I actually yelled at a patient. The sisters brought a mother and child to the Children's Home. The child had kwashiorkor and around his eyelashes was a pink outline. The corneas of his eyes were opaque with ulcers in the middle. He had

* Estimates vary from 20% to 50%.

severe Vitamin A deficiency. I had had a terrible day and this was the last thing I wanted to see – a permanently blind baby.

"How many children do you have?" I barked in Creole.

"Eight."

"Do you have a husband."

"No"

The cumulative frustration of seeing hoards of unhelpable children poured out of my mouth.

"Why do you have babies when you can't feed them?

"Do you realize your child is blind?"

"You need to stop having sex."

Her face did not change expression as I humiliated her, and after realizing what I had just done I decided to quit for the day.

This emotional outburst was unfair, as many women, unable to support their families, are forced into prostitution, the only work they can find. They continue to have unprotected intercourse, generating more mouths to feed.

The men are polygamous, with powerful and successful men taking more than one wife. Having many children is a sign of virility and some of my male patients bragged about it. I made the mistake of asking how many were still alive only once; after that, I did not want to know. As in virtually all societies, the ability to attract many women greatly enhanced a male's prestige. It also kept the women disciplined, as this Haitian proverb illustrates:

> Fanm jalou pa janm vini gwo.
> Jealous women never become fat.

Women were obligated to have sex and more than once I saw beaten women who had not consented. They looked as if their faces had been used as punching bags, with swollen eyelids, ballooned lips and split, bruised skin. They did not appear to be bitter, giving me the impression that they accepted it as a sex-related hazard. Once in a while they would be accompanied by the man who hit them, affording me the opportunity to unleash a verbal tirade. It did not change anything, but at least it made me feel good. In the United States, I would never yell when a man beat a woman; it is considered inappropriate moralizing.

Sex was considered as a biological rather than an emotional function. Unemployment was high, boredom rife and as one man put it, "There's nothing else to do." When there is a blackout in a American city, there is no television and people have nothing to do but go to bed. Nine months later, the babies arrive. In Haiti, the babies are always coming, as if there is a permanent blackout.

The Haitians were not shy about sex. Anytime I took a date to the beach, the Haitian men, upon ascertaining that I spoke Creole, would ask me how much I wanted to allow them to sleep with her. They had no qualms about asking me about her anatomical details – never considering that these questions were rude. The lyrics of popular songs that blared over the radio would even make a lawyer for the American Civil Liberties Union blush. By far the most popular was a song that had the lyrics:

> Pi gwo, pi long, pi apetisan
> Wider, longer and more appetizing

This phallic reference blared all through Port-au-Prince and was also on many bumper stickers. While it would be easy to blame Haiti's rapid growth rate on promiscuity and irresponsibility, the underlying problem was the same as all the other problems – economic. Children represented the best investment for those who had no sense of economic security. As the Haitian proverb goes:

> Pitit se richès pòv malere.
> Children are the riches of the poor.

Unlike in the United States, where children rarely produce economically before age 16, a child in Haiti was useful by age 4, carrying water, harvesting crops and watching other children. Many children in the slums and countryside worked twelve hours a day. They represented security in old age and since so many of them died, one could never have enough.

While in Haiti I became convinced that improved health care was an illusion unless overpopulation was addressed. I could not see how these immensely complex problems of malnutrition, poor sanitation, and poverty could be solved while masses of children were being produced. Since the order I was working with was Catholic, I respected their views and did not attempt to do family planning, although several of the sisters surreptitiously told me that they thought that was what Haiti needed.

I did have the opportunity to do family planning while working with a non-sectarian Dutch organization. I also met doctors, missionaries and international family planning experts who inundated me with a variety of views on how to handle the problem. From this, I regretfully came to the conclusion that lowering the birth rate in Haiti in a short period of time would not be possible without totalitarian methods that would be morally reprehensible.

The government distributes condoms and birth control pills at low prices, but they are mainly used by a small educated minority. The illiterate superstitious poor simply do not have the education or discipline to use them.

In Haiti, Mardi Gras is a week of total debauchery and hedonism, where an entire country forgets its woes and enjoys life to the fullest. Nine months later, the babies arrive. The government wisely tries to use this occasion for education. Family planning T-shirts were distributed free. On the front they had a picture of a man, woman and child, while on the back they depicted a method of birth control. One showed a picture of a condom and said:

> Ak kapòt, se sa nèt.
> With a condom, it is complete.

Many people walked around with these shirts but when I asked them what they said, they had no idea. I would explain to them the message of the shirt and they would politely listen, humoring me with their attention and going along their way.

Trying to dispense condoms was an exercise in futility. The Haitian men had a great disdain for them. When I treated venereal disease I would dispense condoms, since I knew that having my patients refrain from sex was not a viable possibility. Most men took them politely, but one time a patient became indignant, jeering at me and asking if I used them. I had assaulted his macho self-image. Although I saw over 10,000 patients while I was in Haiti, this was the only time one was ever rude with me.

Once a patient asked me for a condom, and being suspicious, I asked her why.

"My children use them as balloons."

She was right. I often saw kids using a blown-up condom as a soccer balls. This was the main use of condoms in Haiti.

Oral contraceptives did not fare much better. I rarely gave them, because I felt uncomfortable exposing my patients to the many possible complications without being able to monitor their blood chemistries, especially their liver functions. However, I frequently cared for patients who had received them from another source and now appeared before me for their prenatal check-ups.

"M' pa gen san", "I don't have blood," one told me. I finally figured out after about ten minutes that this meant she had missed her period. There were at least five words in Creole for period and it seemed to me that each woman only knew one of them.

The story was always the same. The patient did not understand that they had to take the pills every day, whether they were having sexual relations or not. No matter how often I repeated this, explained the menstral cycle, drew pictures, whatever, I could not get my patients to comply with this simple regimen.

I spoke with one missionary, a nurse, who implanted IUD's (intrauterine device) as a method of birth control and felt this was the wave of the future in Haiti, since no patient participation was required. IUD's are coiled pieces of plastic or metal that are placed inside the uterus, disrupting the uterine wall and preventing the implantation of a fertilizied egg. Once considered an effective method of birth control, IUD's have fallen into disrepute in the United States because they can cause permanent sterilization from an associated pelvic infection which is invariably followed by a million-dollar lawsuit.

This nurse told me that she had no complications with this method of birth control, but that was not my experience. One woman came to Sans Fil with abdominal pain and fevers. Unsure of her diagnosis, I treated her with antibiotics in case she had typhoid. What concerned me was that she was not a typical Sans Fil patient as she was well-nourished and attired in new clothes.

The next day, she was worse, profusely sweating with exquisite tenderness in all areas of her abdomen. I was afraid she had a surgical emergency such as appendicitis, but since I did not have the equipment to treat it I just gave her a high dose of pain-killers and told the sister to try to arrange that she be taken to the Hôpital Général. Several minutes later, while I was examining another patient, this patient called "Doktè Joe, Doktè Joe."

I returned to her bedside and she showed me a foul-smelling, blood-covered piece of plastic; her IUD had fallen out. Now everything made sense. I found some rubber gloves and lubricant and proceded to perform a pelvic examination. I explained everything to her and she was cooperative until my fingers probed deep inside of her and pressed on her cervix, the entrance to the uterus through which the IUD had been placed. At this point she emitted a loud shriek. This is all I wanted to know. She had a positive "Chandelier sign," so-called because movement of the uterus is so painful, the patient jumps for the chandelier. It is diagnostic of PID, pelvic inflammatory disease, which is when the uterus and surrounding structures become infected.

Her case did not entirely make sense, because PID caused by IUD's often has no symptoms. Perhaps her IUD had perforated the uterine wall causing peritonitis, or maybe she had an ectopic pregnancy, which occurs when the fertilized egg implants in its transport tube instead of the uterus itself. Ectopic pregnancies are another complication of IUD's.

The sisters took her to the Hôpital Général but the staff refused to admit her, which took a lot of chutzpah, since they were the ones who had implanted the IUD. There was not much I could do except add another antibiotic. Over the next two weeks she languished while I helplessly manipulated her antibiotics, hoping I could hit on the right combination. I never did, and she died, forcing me to wonder whether it was fair to put these things in people when they did not have access to the medical care to treat complications. I saw several patients like her who did not die, but during my stay in Haiti I never implanted a single IUD.

Another missionary I met felt she was working with the wave of the future in Third-World birth control – injectable estrogens. The most common of these is Depo-Provera, which is employed extensively in Southeast Asia. Because it has rendered some women sterile, the Federal Drug administration has prohibited its use in the United States. She injected many women in northern Haiti with good results and was of the opinion that the medical risks were negligible when compared to unbridled population growth.

One missionary, an attractive, unattached 22-year-old, had a completely different approach. A fundamentalist, she believed that the Haitians needed to be taught Christian values, complaining that they had too much "illicit sex." I did not see how this was possible, since sex was the only fun many of these poor people had. I did not argue with her, though, since it would not change her mind. However, she lost her credibility with me when she called me several months later.

"Joe, can you do a pregnancy test for me?"

I guess the Haitians converted her.

One method of birth control that is natural but effective is prolonged breast feeding. Breast-feeding is nature's method of birth control because it causes a hormone to be excreted that inhibits ovulation. A sexually-active woman who nurses her child at regular intervals including at night has only a 5% chance of becoming pregnant per month as opposed to 25% in a woman who is not breast-feeding. In one African tribe, the !Kung, women breast-feed their children until they are three and subsequently have much lower birth rates.

The problem is that in Haiti either the mothers are too malnourished to breast feed or an outside organization gives them food for their children, resulting in decreased milk production. This increases the chance of pregnancy. Also, the avoidance of breast-feeding is a sign of upward mobility, a behavior encouraged by corporations who distributed artificial milk prepartions to widen their markets. Thus it is unlikely that nature's birth control will be a major factor in controlling Haiti's population.

USAID, the United States Agency for International Development, had a family planning division and I was fortunate enough to have the opportunity to speak to its director. A pleasant man of about 50, he did not have the burnt-out look of most other international development workers, although he had been doing this type of work for most of his professional life. He just did not have unrealistic expectations.

He smiled warmly as I aired my frustrations in trying to cure malnutrition in single-parent families of six with no source of income, my limited success in distributing condoms, and the terrible side effects I had seen from IUD's. I was obviously not the first distraught physician he had ever heard. His avuncular approach did not mean he did not realize the urgency of the problem, and his office was filled with charts and graphs of worldwide population trends confirming the dire predictions of thirty years ago.

He told me that working with the Haitian government was challenging, as it is difficult to convince a people that there are too many of their kind. It requires tact and diplomacy. Third-World countries view attempts by the industrialized world to decrease their population as a subtle form of genocide. After having their resources stripped by multinational corporations, the wealthy gaze back at the consequent economic catastrophe and pontificate that there are too many people for limited resources or whine about the ozone layer.

He disagreed with me when I told him that I felt many Haitians were not interested in birth control, implying that I was not patient enough. He told me that the use of contraception is actually decreasing in Haiti, so that now only 10% of the women were using it. However, he pointed out that his research had indicated that almost half of the women would use it if it were available. He saw it as a distribution problem caused by a lack of funds.

Whether access to contraception would improve the situation is debatable. I met one Catholic priest who had worked in Haiti for 10 years. He was quite liberal and did not have strong philosophical and theological objections to birth control, but he felt access to it would not make a major dent in the birth rate, pointing out that similar so-called advances in American ghetto populations not only did not lower birth rates, but may have contributed to their rise.

I left Haiti convinced that its burgeoning population was its greatest problem. Of the hodgepodge of solutions – increased access to birth control, teaching responsible behavior, economic development – none seemed to address the problem's urgency. Perhaps the day will come when masses of Third-World populations are subjected to forced sterilization and abortion programs like China and India. The present one-child policy of China is resulting in female infanticide because a male child represents more economic security that a female one. In the future China will have an under-supply of females to marry – which could cause social upheaval. Although I personally could never agree to this, I would not be surprised if drastic birth control measures became commonplace.

Chapter 9

Jonas Salk Would Cry

Maladi pa konn bon.
Illness does not avoid the good.

Haitian Proverb

Day, Nick and I were having lunch at Sans Fil when one of the volunteer nurses frantically interrupted us. A patient she had been feeding was choking to death. We ran to the men's ward and saw poor Yves lying in his bed, managing a weak cough as a gurgling sound emanated from his throat. His eyes were bulging, his lips were ashen blue, and his ubiquitous smile gave way to a look of terror.

We sat him up and I wrapped my arms firmly around his abdomen, digging my left thumb directly below his breast bone. I squeezed hard, pulling my fist upward into his diaphragm – the Heimlich maneuver. Yves's mouth opened, allowing a gust of air and several pieces of rice to fly out. The gurgling stopped, the frantic gasps abated, and after several anxious minutes, a huge smile crossed his face.

Crippled from polio, Yves was not a quadriplegic but a "pentaplegic" meaning that not only were his arms and legs paralyzed, but also his neck. When he sat in a chair, his head had to be propped up because he could not hold it straight.

Along with his arm and leg muscles, his facial muscles had atrophied, so that his eyes appeared to bulge out of his face. Even worse, the polio had affected the muscles that controlled swallowing, so he frequently aspirated his food.

Yves was the most popular patient at Sans Fil. Every day, volunteers would fight to feed him. He sat in a chair with several rosaries around his neck, smiling. I was amazed how someone paralyzed, incontinent, and impotent could be so content. I told everyone to only feed Yves while he was sitting and to grind up his food. Since this instruction was often ignored, Yves occasionally needed the Heimlich maneuver to expel beans and rice from his windpipe.

The will to live was the only thing keeping Yves alive. Patients like him usually die from pneumonia because they aspirate their germ-infested saliva. He got pneumonia several times but responded brilliantly when I started him on antibiotics. My main fear was that he would contract an antibiotic-resistant pneumonia, but fortunately this never happened.

Polio is caused by a virus that usually results in a minor illness with fever and diarrhea. However, in 1% of the cases, the virus attacks the nerve cells in the spinal cord that control muscle movement, thus paralyzing the muscles. The virus can even attack the nerve cells that innervate the facial and swallowing muscles, as in Yves' case. Polio may leave only one limb paralyzed or it can paralyze the entire body. There is no treatment, even when it is diagnosed immediately.

In keeping with the tradition of abandoning unwanted children to nuns, someone dropped off a child at the Children's Home. Only two years old, she was neatly dressed in a fresh blue dress with a pressed white collar. Her hair, which had red and black bands, was neatly braided and tied with two white ribbons. She even had underwear, a luxury for Haitian children, and on her feet were immaculate white socks and polished shoes. There was no dirt under her fingernails. Whoever abandoned her wanted us to know that they cared for her.

Patricia, as I named her, smiled trustingly as I examined her. She had only one problem – she could not move her legs. I moved them for her, noting that they were not rigid but pliable – a flaccid paralysis. Using the handle of a metal spoon, I firmly scratched the bottom of her foot. Normally, the toes should turn down but in Patricia, they fanned out and the big toe turned up. This is an abnormal reflex – the Babinski sign in medical parlance – and usually indicates irreversible neurological damage, a prediction the next several months proved to be correct.

Patricia had acute polio. When I told this to an American nurse who was visiting, she began to cry. Polio typically causes less neurological damage in children, so that Patricia was only a paraplegic; unlike poor Yves, who had contracted polio when he was twenty and had more devastating neurological sequelae. The sisters sent Patricia to an organization that cared for many of Haiti's handicapped.

Unfortunately, there are more handicapped people in Haiti than this organization could possibly handle, because few Haitians are immunized. Ever since the United States led the successful assault against the disease that crippled Franklin Roosevelt, polio has been systematically eliminated in the industrialized world. But the transfer of this simple technology to Haiti has been slow. Only 7% of Haiti has been immunized against polio, a national tragedy. As a result, the streets are full of paraplegic beggars crawling around, doomed to a life of degradation and dependence.

Haiti was replete with terrible diseases that could be prevented by vaccination. One day the sisters asked me to see a a patient who had just arrived at Sans Fil. Antoine, a muscular twenty-year old, lay on the concrete floor with his back arched like a wrestler trying to avoid being pinned. His abdominal muscles were taut, as were the facial muscles, giving him a smile that appeared to be plastered on his face.

One of the other patients helped me and we picked up his contorted body and placed him in bed. He could not speak, only murmur gutteral sounds in a frustrated attempt to communicate.

"What a waste," I thought to myself as I examined him, probing his rock hard body with my fingers and checking his skin for wounds or cuts. I took one of his feet in my hand, pushed it towards his head, and released it. It started to flap rapidly—a phenomena called "clonus." Antoine had a classic presentation of tetanus. He had several infected skin wounds, any one of which could have been the entrance site of the Clostridium tetani, the causative bacillus.

The bacteria remain localized to the wound but they manufacture a toxin that attacks the nerves and causes them to continuously fire, resulting in constant muscle contraction. The muscles along the spinal column were contracting with such force that they arched his back and his artificial smile, called "risus sardonicus" or "sardonic smile," was caused by his contracted facial muscles. He also had lockjaw, the characteristic first symptom of tetanus, rendering him speechless.

Tetanus is rare in the United States, but is seen among religious sects that refuse immunization, such as the Amish. Death is frequent, even with intensive treatment, because of pneumonia. I felt sure Antoine would die like other cases of tetanus I had treated in Haiti, but I was obliged to give him a chance.

First I cleaned his wounds with alcohol and then started an intravenous line for hydration and Penicillin. I personally purchased the tetanus antiserum from a Haitian pharmacy and administered it. This does not reverse the neurological damage, but prevents the tetanus from spreading. I placed a nasogastric tube, and for the next three weeks Antoine's sole cuisine was reconstituted powdered milk. He received daily doses of Valium to relax his tightened muscles.

To my amazement, Antoine began to improve. Daily, I coached him, telling him to keep fighting. The lockjaw was the first to resolve, enabling him to eat without the nasogastric tube. Soon he was able to sit up with help, and five weeks after he arrived he could stand. In tetanus, the muscle contractions resolve spontaneously in a month if the patient does not succumb to the plethora of other complications – secondary infections, pneumonia, heart arrhythmias, blood pressure instability. The sisters thought it was a miracle, a claim I could not dispute since his respiratory muscles were spared. Otherwise it would have meant certain death as no respirator was available. Equally unbelievable, he had no permanent damage. He thanked me profusely for my help and then left, able to return to his job of pulling carts loaded with charcoal.

Although it was disturbing to see tetanus ravaging adults, nothing was more heartrending than when it afflicted an infant. The Haitian midwives cut the umbilical cord of newborns with a soiled knife and then pack the stump with animal dung to stop the bleeding, an outstanding way of transmitting tetanus. One missionary told me about a woman who brought her twelfth child to her clinic with tetanus. The baby died and the missionary told the mother that the person who cut the cord killed her baby. When the mother had number thirteen, she returned with her infant still attached to the placenta and had the missionary cut the umbilical cord. Education programs to reduce neonatal tetanus have had moderate success, but since many Haitians are not vaccinated, tetanus tragically persists.

A mother appeared at the Children's Home with her plump, gorgeous six-month-old daughter who had been having fevers and seizures. Her tiny hands were unbreakably clenched, and her arms formed the highway over which her arched back made a bridge. Her feet were flexed forward so that they appeared like those of a pirouetting ballerina.

Her bright eyes alertly followed me as I looked for the wound that precipitated her disease. I found none. It was like examining a warped board, her body remaining rigid so that when I probed her abdomen, someone had to hold her so she would not tip over. She began to cry, tears streaming down her face while a loud hum emanated from her throat. She could not open her mouth. I tried to pry it open, but her lockjaw was so strong that I broke my tongue depressor. I treated her like Antoine, with Penicillin, tetanus antitoxin and nasogastric feeding, but the paralysis affected her respiratory muscles. She struggled to breathe for two days while I kept her well-hydrated and fed, but pneumonia and respiratory failure ended her short life.

While polio and tetanus had more spectacular presentations, it was the lowly measles that killed the most. Mass immunization programs against it began in the industrialized world in the early 1960's. Prior to this time few children escaped this annoying affliction because it is highly contagious. It begins like a typical cold – cough, fever, conjunctivitis and runny nose – which is then followed by a blotchy rash that starts on the face and spreads over the body. I had seen several cases in the United States, but these patients did well, giving me the fallacious impression that it was a benign disease. I discovered otherwise.

In a nourished patient, the complications of measles such as pneumonia, diarrhea, and brain infections may ensue, but they are rare. The debilitated Haitians were not so lucky. Measles attacked them at a younger age and often caused a diarrhea that lasted for weeks, and the subsequent malabsorption turned mild marasmus into fatal kwashiorkor. Conjunctivitis diminished the eyes' ability to manufacture tears and this, compounded with Vitamin A deficiency, accelerated opacification of the corneas, resulting in blindness.

Measles is contagious in the early stages before the rash appears, making its diagnosis difficult; thus several epidemics would sweep through the Children's Home before I realized what was happening. Even when the rash appeared, it was hard to diagnosis in black patients. Fortunately, measles causes a peculiar inflammation of the gums, a raised red blotch with a white dot in the middle, the so-called "Koplik spot," that is unique to the disease. Daily, I looked at the gums of any child with a cold. When I diagnosed measles, I immediately discharged the child.

Knowing the brutal consequences of the lack of immunizations, I gave first priority to establishing a vaccination program. While the number of people I would immunize would be small, if I prevented one person from contracting these horrible diseases, it would be worth it.

The vaccines, donated by the United States, are distributed free by the government. The problem is obtaining them. Few Haitian bureaucrats can be accused of being workaholics. Their offices are open from 9 to 3 which in actuality translates to 10 to 2 with 11 to 1 being for lunch. When coffee breaks are included, this leaves little time for actual work.

Since I had not learned Creole yet, I hired an ambitious young man to translate. Like many uneducated Haitians, he had learned English loitering at the hotels. After three days of hassles, paperwork, and pleading, I obtained the three necessary vaccines: the oral polio vaccine; "DPT" which stands for diphtheria, pertussis (whooping cough) and tetanus; and "MMR" for mumps, measles and rubella.

There is more to giving vaccines than simply lining up children and injecting them. Vaccines can have complications, especially in the sick and malnourished, causing rash, fevers, and, in rare instances, neurological complications such as permanent paralysis. First I vaccinated those who were healthy in the Children's Home and, fortunately, I never saw any serious side effects.

Armed with this experience, I was ready to start vaccinating at the clinics. Day and Nick enthusiastically agreed to run the program. We gave DPT to all the children between the ages of 2 months and 6 years and MMR to all children between 10 months and 6 years. Giving these vaccines to those over 6 years old may do more harm than good, since anyone who has survived this long in Haiti has probably acquired natural immunity. They received only the polio vaccine.

Most of the vaccines except the MMR needed to be admininstered three times to assure complete efficacy. This was the hard part, because not all Haitians understood the need for repeat doses even though we gave them cards indicating when to return. Many never returned for their booster shots, but it was not a major loss, since 80% obtained immunity with just a single dose.

I was euphoric when we finally had the program in full swing. The first time this happened was at one of the clinics. Nick and Day sat interviewing the mothers, asking them if they had had previous immunizations for their children. I looked them over quickly to make sure that the children were healthy enough to tolerate the vaccine. Then we gave them the vaccines, first the injection of DPT which made them cry so that the oral polio vaccine was easily dropped into their mouths. Ideally, we needed an immunization gun but since it was not available, we used the 1 cc syringes that a medical supply company had donated. We had so many syringes that we could dispose of a syringe after a single use, thus preventing the spread of disease.

Eventually, Nick and Day ran the program independently. By the time we were done, we had immunized over 2000 babies and children, thus preventing untold misery.

I was bragging to some friends about our program over a couple of beers in Pétionville. One of them was Michel, who was from France and a member of the French equivalent of the Peace Corps. He now called himself an "international consultant" and had long given up doing anything meaningful in Haiti and instead concentrated on seducing women of as many different ethnic backgrounds as possible.

"Where did you get the vaccines, Joe?", he asked in perfect English.

"From the government," I replied, while wondering what he was getting at.

He laughed.

"Joe, those vaccines sit in customs for weeks without being refrigerated. They are inactive."

Chapter 10

Questions without Answers

There is no human life not worth living.

Albert Schweitzer

The child was lying naked on a bench, abandoned by its parents at one of the clinics. As I glanced at him, green diarrhea jetted out of his rectum. His deeply sunken eyes, tearless cry and parched mouth confirmed his dehydrated state. Although only one-year-old, he was going to die unless he was taken to the Children's Home.

When I looked at his eyes, I was horrified to find that both his pupils were white instead of black – he had cataracts. In an adult the removal of a cataract restores vision, but this child had congenital cataracts. Contrary to popular belief, one does not see with the eyes but with the brain, the eyes merely acting as cameras to transmit the image. If the brain does not learn to see while it is developing during infancy, it never learns to see. Therefore, this child would remain blind, even if the cataracts were removed. What would he do in Haiti?

The sisters brought him to the Children's Home, I rehydrated him intravenously, and within two days the diarrhea stopped. He ate like a little pig and soon appeared healthy, except that he had the annoying habits of banging his head against the side rails, smashing his face with his hands and rolling face down on his bed. This bizarre behavior was self-stimulation that compensated for his blindness.

Before coming to Haiti, I spoke with a prosperous physician forty years my senior. I told him all my ambitious plans – saving dehydrated babies, starting a vaccination program, setting up a laboratory – saving lives, the supposed goal of medicine.

He looked at me with the omniscient condescension that typifies the relationship between older and younger physicians and remarked, "You will destroy the ecological balance."

When he saw the shocked look on my face, he felt bad and retreated from his visceral reply, wishing me luck and asking what he could do to help.

After curing this patient, I realized that he had a point. Medically I had cured this child, but did I have access to the resources to rehabilitate him, teach him braille, educate him, teach him a marketable trade and finally, find him a job?

Of course not. I just got him better.

Perhaps the sisters could find some benevolent organization to care for him. But what if they did not? Would he end up begging on the street like so many others – until he died of starvation or illness?

Did I do him a favor?

Is Albert Schweitzer right?

If I decided to save his life, did I have the responsibility to arrange his care for the next seventy years? If I were unable to assume this responsibility, should I have allowed nature to take its course, select out the weak and preserve the "ecological balance?"

Perhaps his case would not have caused me so much consternation if I had not just met Pierre, a new patient at Sans Fil. At a young age, Pierre was crippled by a rare complication of tuberculosis that collapsed his vertebrae, thus damaging his spinal cord. His mother, unable to care for him, gave him to a missionary group that washed him, fed him, taught him English and converted him to Christianity.

Unfortunately for Pierre, this group decided to spread the Lord's word in another country, leaving him homeless. A relative tried to care for him but could not, so Pierre ended up lying on the street for several months until a priest found him and brought him to Sans Fil.

When he first arrived, he was covered with flies that were feasting on the multiple skin erosions caused by two months of immobilization.

His legs and arms were frozen at ninety-degree angles, his muscles having contracted from disuse. His deformed back arched into a huge dowager hump, its apex being at the same level as his earlobes. He smiled as I examined him, but was too weak to speak. It was this image I recalled while saving the blind infant.

Day and Nick recognized his strong will to live and went to work – rehydrating him, debriding his skin ulcers, and exercising his limbs. His legs did not fully recover, but his arms did, so that after a month, Pierre was sitting in a wheelchair, dispensing advice to anyone who would listen – the sage of Sans Fil.

Pierre enjoyed imitating my speaking Creole. Like most Haitians, he found it amusing not only because of my heavy accent but because I spoke like a peasant. Upper-class Haitians speak Creole interwoven with the euphonious glissandos of French, but the peasants speak the same language with a guttural twang. Having never studied French and with Haitian peasants as my teachers, I spoke it the same way. It was as if a European learned English while working in an American ghetto and consequently spoke jive. Americans would find it funny.

Pierre was not only a gifted mimic, but also a talented artist and the drawings he gave me are among my personal treasures. His command of English and repertoire of hymns made him popular with the visitors. He showed me what untapped ability existed in the poorest of the poor – even the handicapped – if they were only given a chance. Perhaps the blind baby would prove to have hidden talents also, but the thought of that poor child ending up as Pierre did when I first saw him made me shudder. I knew that chances were that there would be no angel in white to help. I convinced myself I had done the right thing in saving the blind baby, but if someone had told me he was better off dead, I would have disagreed – but not vehemently.

The most agonizing decision was whether to treat those who were brain-damaged by meningitis. It was a disease I could not miss because the stakes were so high. It could be fatal, but, even worse, it could cause irreversible brain damage, condemning a child to grovel on the streets until death came. Classically, these children had a piercing high-pitched cry, a bulging fontanelle, fevers and no appetite. Unfortunately, meningitis usually presented with much subtler symptoms, such as lethargy or persistent crying. I did at least two spinal taps daily and was constantly amazed at how subtle the symptoms of meningitis could be. Although diagnosing a case of meningitis early was satisfying, it was more the exception than the norm. Many of the cases I saw were like Louis.

I first saw Louis at a clinic where his perplexed mother told me, "Li pa ka pale", "He can't speak." Louis looked about four-years-old and even the developmentally-delayed Haitian children speak by this age. It made no sense to me until I looked carefully at his face. When Louis stared at me, the eyebrow above one eye furrowed while the other remained motionless. One half of his face was completely lifeless so that attempts to smile or cry resulted in macabre half-face expressions. When I examined him further, I discovered he could not move one side of his body. I had seen this in the United States many times, but only in the elderly; Louis had suffered a stroke.

Suspecting meningitis, I took him to the Children's Home and confirmed my diagnosis with a spinal tap. With intravenous antibiotics, the meningitis cleared, but the stroke did not. Because he could pathetically move only one side of his body, he could no longer walk, and when he tried to speak an incoherent gibberish came out. The stroke had destroyed the speech center of his brain, thus explaining the mother's original complaint. The sisters offered to care for him, but the mother insisted on taking him back. He had absolutely no chance of surviving with even a minimum of dignity.

I had encountered this scenario several times. I cured a brain-damaged infant from meningitis, but the neurological deficits persisted. Instead of these children's dying, they were being returned to their families paralyzed, retarded and unable to communicate. Was I doing these children a favor?

It was obvious that I was not. Supposedly the neurological deficits of meningitis resolve when the disease is cured, but I never saw this happen. Eventually, I stopped antibiotics on any child with meningitis who had brain damage, effectively allowing him to die. I do not know if it was the right decision, but it is the one I made. It was classic situation ethics. In the United States, where there were programs for rehabilitation and special education, it would have been wrong to withhold treatment. In Haiti, it was a different situation.

Many who tried to help Haiti concluded that the only way to help a handicapped Haitian was to get him out of the country. I was no exception; but as I was to find out, this often did more harm than good.

At Sans Fil, there were two prime candidates – Mario, who had a heart defect, and Antoine, who had a unhealable leg ulcer.

Mario's heart failure was so severe that it resulted in massive total body swelling, so that his legs looked like tree trunks, his abdomen like a watermelon and his face like a full moon. Even more striking than his appearance was the constant Whoosh, Whoosh, Whoosh emanating from his chest. He had a heart murmur so loud that I could hear it while standing at his bedside! I placed my hand in his chest and felt the murmur reverberate through my bones from his breastbone to the side of his rib cage. I listened to his chest with my stethoscope, hearing a heart murmur that was literally deafening.

Mario had either a defective heart valve or a hole in one of the walls that separates the heart's chambers. I did not know which it was, but I did know this – there was nothing I could do about it. He required heart surgery. I had Day and Nick give him Digoxin and Lasix, which allowed him to breath easier. However, he slowly worsened to the point where it required a herculean effort on his part just to walk to the bathroom. I reconciled in my mind that my job was to keep him comfortable during his stay of execution.

The other was Antoine, a handsome, charming and somewhat manipulative young man with a huge leg ulcer that refused to heal. We cleaned it, debrided it, dressed it, gave him sundry antibiotics and accomplished nothing. Antoine needed a skin graft, a procedure I had neither the expertise nor the equipment to perform. Without one, Antoine would eventually need to have his leg amputated.

Along came American technology in the form of a visiting doctor from a prestigious hospital. He examined Mario and Antoine and decided to arrange proper medical care for them in the United States. Day went to work pulling the proper strings in the Haitian bureaucracy. He had to physically carry Mario to a police station to get him fingerprinted. It took him a month of forging birth certificates, paying bribes, and taking pictures, and culminated in his posing as an American doctor in the Office of the Director General, an equivalent to a cabinet post in the United States.

It paid off. Day obtained passports and visas for both Mario and Antoine. The three of them along with Nick left for the United States – the last frontier for the Haitians. Mario, his face more swollen than ever, smiled and waved a Haitian flag as I watched him being wheeled onto the airplane.

The American doctors were impressed that we had kept Mario alive. Even his blood Digoxin level was the proper concentration. They performed a cardiac catheterization, a procedure in which dye is injected into the heart and X-rays are taken. It showed that Mario had a defective pulmonary valve.

Mario, who one week ago had lived in a country where most medical problems are handled by oungans prescribing herbs, was wheeled into a sterile operating suite where the best and brightest placed him in the proper plane of anesthesia, and cut open his chest. His heart was dramatically stopped and he was placed on one of the triumphs of medical technology, the heart-lung machine which kept him alive while his pulmonary valve was replaced.

Mario would have been better off with an oungan. His heart was too weak from its long fight to keep him alive; its muscle fibers stretched beyond the point where they could muster a decent contraction. Merely replacing the valve could not change this. His lungs filled with fluid and Mario found himself with a tube jammed down his throat while a machine breathed for him, wondering what he had done to offend God to deserve this.

Mario languished in the cardiac intensive care unit for a week with tubes in every orifice and needles in his arteries and veins. Finally he died the American way – in a blaze of glory – with interns dramatically pounding his chest and shocking his heart, while pushing a potpourri of drugs into his blood vessels. Antoine, with his healing leg, attended his funeral.

Upon hearing about Mario's death, I consoled myself in the knowledge that Antoine was cured and now had a chance in the industrialized world. Alas, poor Antoine had no more chance of adapting to the Midwest than a Midwesterner who found himself alone in rural Haiti. No one knew his language and no one understood his culture. He became disgusted and depressed, and returned to Haiti – but at least with two good legs.

These attempts to help represented the ultimate in frustration. After $100,000 in medical care, Mario was dead and Antoine was once again in the environment that spawned his initial state. Again, I tried to console myself by thinking we at least gave publicity to the plight of Haiti, but deep down I felt it was a colossal waste. It represented a sensationalist approach to a difficult problem.

How many vaccinations could have been given with that money?

How many could have been educated?

Those who brought high-tech American medicine to Haiti caused problems, too. Frequently, I saw cases where surgery did not help the patient. One middle-aged woman came to the clinic complaining of "feblès" or "weakness." This is the most common complaint and is usually due to malnutrition. She cheerfully answered my questions, telling me she had been selling fruit at one of the local markets, but in the past month had had to stop because she was constantly tired. A drab blue plaid dress hung from her feeble frame and a multicolored handkerchief covered her head. Her most striking feature, though, was her bulging eyes, unintentionally staring at me – a classic presentation of hyperthyroidism.

The thyroid is a gland located in the neck in front of the trachea or windpipe. It secretes hormones, chemical messengers, that regulate the body's metabolism. Too much thyroid hormone increases the metabolic rate so that hyperthyroid patients become overactive, nervous and irritable. They sweat constantly, which makes their skin moist, and they have high blood pressure. Their reflexes become so active that a doctor checking them can accidentally get kicked in the groin. Frequently, collagen is deposited behind the eyes, causing them to bulge, making them appear like they are constantly staring.

Her problem did not make sense to me because hyperthyroid patients rarely complain of weakness. If anything, they complain of having too much energy. The situation became more puzzling when I examined her. Her skin was extremely dry, her blood pressure was low and when I tapped under her kneecaps with my hammer, she barely had any reflexes. This seemingly contradictory presentation was explained by a 3-inch circumferential scar stretched across the front of her neck. With the exception of the bulging eyes, she had all the symptoms of hypothyroidism.

"Did you have an operation there?", I asked in Creole.

"Yes," she replied, "About a year ago."

"Why did they operate?" I continued.

She did not know, telling me that an American surgeon had operated on her at a local mission hospital. Apparently, the surgeon had partially removed her thyroid gland, making her hypothyroid. Since the collagen behind her eyes did not regress, they still bulged. If she had been in the United States, there would have been no problem. The blood level of the thyroid hormones would have been monitored periodically. If they became too low, the hormone would have been replaced orally.

In Haiti, it is not that easy. This poor woman had no idea what her problem was. If she did have follow-up, she chose to ignore it, perhaps not comprehending the directions given to her. I had no thyroid medicine and was unable to help her. All surgeons know that performing an operation properly is only half the battle; meticulous postoperative care is also necessary. Failure to do so can ruin everything.

Nowhere is this more evident than in eye surgery. Several organizations bring sophisticated equipment such as expensive operating microscopes with the noblest of intentions: to make the blind see. One university even sends training physicians to learn how to remove cataracts and perform corneal transplants. Haitians who had eye surgery often came to me for other medical reasons. I noticed that the surgery performed was technically good, but there was one problem. The patient could not see.

A cataract is a lens that opacifies, blocking vision. The lens is located behind the iris, the colored part of the eye that encircles the pupil. It bends light rays so that they focus clearly on the back of the eye, or retina. The lens may become a cataract for many reasons, such as diabetes, trauma or simply old age. When it does, there is only one treatment: removal. Primitive societies used to stick thorns into the eye, pushing the cataract out of the line of vision. Unfortunately, the ensuing infection destroyed the entire eye.

With modern surgical techniques, a cataract can be removed safely. However, there is nothing to bend the light rays in the eye so that they focus clearly on the retina. More than an operation is needed. The eye must be watched for complications, and after the incisions have healed, the proper spectacles must be prescribed to compensate for the absent lens. Rarely does this happen in Haiti. Even if patients manage to get the proper glasses, they do not wear them for long. Glasses are a sign of education and prestige to up-and-coming Haitians. A patient with cataract glasses will sell them, opting to see a bowl of food out of focus rather than an empty bowl clearly.

One young man came to my clinic wearing cataract glasses. They are easily identifiable because they are thick and look like miniature magnifying glasses. Since he had never had eye surgery, there was no way he could possibly see with them. I confronted him with this fact, but he denied it. Holding up my watch, I asked "Ki lè li ye," "What time is it?" Grudgingly, he took off his glasses so he could tell me. After I treated his problem, which was a rash, he smiled, thanked me, put on his glasses and left. Giving the façade of education was more important to him than seeing.

Even when we arranged for babies to be adopted overseas, I wondered if we were doing the right thing. A couple I knew, both doctors from Holland, were caring for a sick, malnourished Haitian child in their apartment. As he regained his health, it became apparent that returning "Ti Joseph" to his mother would result in his death, as she had no husband or source of income. The mother was willing to allow Francis and Ann to adopt Ti Joseph, but for a price, $100.

Francis and Ann brooded over this dilemma for weeks. One hundred dollars was a pittance for adding a new life to their family, but they had a philosophical objection to paying the woman, arguing that it would encourage poor Haitians to generate babies for selling. They also wondered about the psychological effect this would have on Ti Joseph when he approached the age of reason and learned the circumstances of his adoption. Francis was not concerned about raising a black child in Holland, proudly recounting the long history of Dutch tolerance to those different from themselves.

An incident solved their dilemma. During the day Francis and Ann worked, so they hired a Haitian nanny for Ti Joseph. One day upon returning, they overheard this woman teaching Ti Joseph his first words. She did not want them to be "mama" or "papa" but "Give me dollar." Ti Joseph's mother was soon $100 richer.

I was involved in a similar situation myself. The sisters had found a woman in the Depot who was almost dead from malnutrition and dehydration, and nursed her back to health. As she improved, it became apparent she was pregnant. I personally saw to it that she got good prenatal care, giving her vitamins and frequent examinations.

Elizabeth was born at two in the morning, but since the phones were not working the sisters could not contact me to deliver her. The next day at Sans Fil, I met this beautiful, healthy baby girl. Two weeks later, she was baptized and I was her "parenn", "godfather."

I saw to it that Elizabeth got the same health care as a yuppie puppie in Manhattan. Minor colds were attacked as if they were life-threatening illnesses and the proper vaccines were administered religiously. I insisted that the mother breast feed her and urged everyone to play with her so that she received proper stimulation. She was gorgeous and looked like a typical healthy American baby although the Haitian women told me she was "gate", "spoiled."

I loved this child almost as if she were my own, and when I realized she would die within weeks after the mother left Sans Fil, I had the same reaction as Francis and Anne – I urged the mother to give Elizabeth to the sisters for adoption. I wondered whether I had the right to do this, but I did it anyway. Working in Haiti was depressing and I needed some positive reinforcement. I was not about to witness the death of a child whom I had been caring for before she was born. The mother, with some coaxing, agreed, and the sisters found the child a home in Belgium. The mother quietly sobbed as the only thing in her life that she loved left her.

I am not sure Elizabeth will appreciate what was done for her when she is 18. She may long to find her mother and this will be difficult, although not impossible, since I have pictures of her. On the other hand, she now has the opportunity to grow up in the industrialized world, get an education and have the luxury of searching for her roots if she so chooses. Perhaps she will decide to help Haiti. However, some day she will read these pages and ask me what gave us the right to take her from her home. I do not know what I will say.

One of the worst aspects of working in Haiti was that I had no backup, unleashing a variety of dilemmas. Frequently a dying patient arrived when I was ready to quit for the day. One Friday evening, after an exhausting week, I was looking forward to meeting some friends at one of the local watering holes. Just as I was walking out of the Children's Home, a woman came towards me. I pretended not to see her and kept walking towards my moped. Undaunted, she held her baby in front of my face and said, "Doktè, li pa vle manje", "Doctor, she won't eat." When I looked at the child, it was obvious why – she was dehydrated and dying.

Earlier in the day, my reaction would have been of compassion but now it was restrained outrage.

"Why did she have to come now?"

"I can't save every baby in this wretched country."

The mother had no job, no husband, no source of income and was pregnant besides. Even if I saved this baby, she would probably die later. It was the same reaction I had during my internship when a new patient came when I was ready to go home. The big difference was that during my internship there was always backup – always someone who could do what I could not. Here there was none. If I jumped on my moped and took off, this child would die.

Even though my emotions were irrational, my actions were not. I had only one choice, and that was to bring the child into the Children's Home and save her. To my surprise, she had a large vein in her hand. In my haste, I perforated it, forming a large hematoma, and therefore had to spend the next half hour finding another vein. When the intravenous line was finally running, I stayed another hour to make sure that the child improved without being overhydrated. The next day, the child was sitting up chewing on a piece of bread and eyeing me suspiciously. The mother, beaming, offered to give her to me.

There were other times, though, when my neglect and fatigue caused a child's death. I had seen Jean in the Children's Home one morning, and since he was only mildly dehydrated, I opted to rehydrate him with a nasogastric tube. I told the sisters I would check on him in the afternoon.

Sans Fil was busy that day, and when I was finally done I realized I was late for a dinner invitation. As I was driving up Rue Delmas, I was debating in my mind whether to check on Jean. I was in the left hand lane to make the turn to the Children's Home when I said to myself, "He'll be all right. He wasn't too dehydrated and surely responded to the oral rehydration. Anyway, the sisters can start an intravenous line if he needs it. I can't be on call 24 hours a day 7 days a week." I veered into the right lane and continued to Pétionville.

This rationalization cost Jean his life. With considerable trepidation, I walked into the Children's Home the next day and immediately headed for Jean. His eyeballs were sunk deep into his skull and his skin tented when I pinched it. His eyes gazed in different directions and when I rubbed my knuckles on his chest, he did not object. The sisters told me he had vomited the fluid and that they could not find a vein to place an intravenous line.

Feeling guilty and remiss, I quickly placed an intravenous line in his scalp and soon had normal saline rushing in. I followed it with ampules of bicarbonate and epinephrine, but it was hopeless. He was too far gone. The fluid continued to pour into his lifeless body until I faced reality and discontinued it. Because I had gone to dinner, this child died.

For the next week, I worked feverishly and compulsively to make up for my error. But I gradually realized that I could not do everything and save everyone. Furthermore, I should not feel guilty about it. Throughout my stay in Haiti, people died because I could not work 24 hours a day. It was just something I had to get used to – the reality of being a physician in Haiti.

Often I had to decide whether to continue treatment or allow someone to die. In the United States, this decision is diffused among other doctors, family, and clergy. In Haiti I had to make it myself. I had to play God.

Day was vigorously sawing the cast off the leg of a young man who had just arrived at Sans Fil. Six weeks previously a car had crashed into him, breaking his femur. The driver just kept going. He had no worry over legal responsibility; he simply saw no sense in helping a stupid peasant who was in his way. Eventually, the injured man had been taken to the Hôpital Général.

Since Day did not have a cast-cutter, he had to use an ancient saw, placing a piece of wood under the cast to prevent cutting the patient. After a half hour, the cast was off. It was as he expected, a disaster. Three inches above the knee, the femur was protruding through the skin. The bone had never been set, just pushed back through the skin and covered with a cast. When the patient did not improve, he was heaved into the Depot. There he lay for several days, getting an occasional bowl of rice until the sisters found him and brought him to Sans Fil.

Day asked me to examine him. I had seen many Depot patients before so nothing surprised me. I walked to the bedside and gazed at a fading human being. Hundreds of large black flies hovered above him, attracted by the excrement he had just deposited on the anticipatory vinyl sheet under him. He preferred to lie on his side, which stabilized his exquisitely painful leg. Bedsores on his ankles and buttocks testified to his recumbent position for the past six weeks. The sisters had cut his hair, as it was infested with lice and scabies.

I asked him what had happened. He babbled incoherently, since he was delirious with fever. Protruding from his thigh was his fractured femur. It was a clean break and I could clearly demarcate the white outer cortex from the red highly-vascular middle. A pungent white frothy pus surrounded the bone. Day pressed on the skin above the bone squeezing out more pus along with feasting maggots. He looked like a refugee from Dachau. The next time a patient in the United States complains to me about the bland hospital food or the lackluster quality of the television picture, I will mention the state of this unfortunate man.

I gazed at him a little longer, then glanced at Day. I said nothing but Day could read my face. I walked away.

A group of idealistic college students was following me. Perceiving my inaction as apathy, they challenged me to save him. One of them suggested that I reset the bone.

This was obviously ridiculous. A broken femur, even in the hands of a skilled orthopedic surgeon, is difficult to reset and must be rejoined by metal plates. I had neither the skill nor the equipment to perform this sophisticated carpentry. Furthermore, if the femur has an infection, it must be eradicated first before any attempt is made to repair him. Day gave him antibiotics, but both of us knew the only way to save him was to amputate the leg. I saw no sense in this. The man had lost his will to live. There is a Haitian proverb that goes:

> Si ou wè msye ale sou li, li pral mouri vre.
> If you see a man soil himself, he will surely die.

This wisdom, well-known to illiterate Haitian peasants, has not percolated up to the American medical establishment. Huge sums are routinely spent on patients trying to die peacefully. After years of practicing medicine, most doctors become less aggressive. In Haiti it took only several months for me to reach this stage. I was no longer the green compulsive intern charging windmills. My medical judgment had aged rapidly. My intervention could not help this man, and to amputate his leg would be an act of macho barbarism.

Day saw to it that he drank well and controlled his pain with generous doses of Demoral, a narcotic. Day tried to feed the poor man, but he had no appetite. After a week, he died peacefully. In Haiti, our job was not only to cure but to comfort.

But sometimes even deciding whether to comfort a patient was difficult. One young man who had come to Sans Fil had a weak smile on his face, the look of some one who has suffered immeasurably and was relieved that he was finally going to die.

"M' ap mouri", "I'm dying," he said between breaths that I timed to be 80 a minute, incompatible with life. His cyanotic lips formed a macabre contrast with his black face. He sat in a green scrub suit, his sweaty palms firmly grasping his knees to stabilize his shoulder girdle. This provided a firm base so the muscles attached to his clavicles could elevate his ribs and aid his labored breathing.

His lips were puckered to increase the oxygen pressure in his lungs, and when he inhaled the force was so great it sucked in the skin between his ribs. He had every symptom of respiratory distress listed in the medical textbooks. In an American hospital, he would have been intubated and placed on a respirator stat.

I listened to his lungs, hoping I would hear something I could treat – the dissonant rales of heart failure which I could eliminate with a diuretic, or the silence of a pleural effusion which I could clear with a thorocentesis. But all I heard was wheezing, the sound made as air whistles and swirls in the huge cavities of vacated lung tissue consumed by endstage tuberculosis.

He read my face, concluded I could not help him, and reaffirmed with a weak smile, "M' ap mouri."

I began anti-tuberculosis drugs and antibiotics, but I did not know how to comfort him. No oxygen was available and I was afraid to administer Demoral or Valium because it might decrease his respiratory drive. It was a terrible dilemma. Should I give him medicine for the comfort that could lead to his demise, or allow him to suffer on the slim hope he would recover? I opted not to give him these medicines. It was the wrong choice. He died the same day, after several more hours of agony.

While working in Haiti taught me a much simpler method of practicing medicine, the ethical complexities were just as difficult as in the United States, where physicians have to deal with decisions on when to discontinue respirators on brain-dead patients and the management of brain-damaged infants who have come out of the womb three months too early. In Haiti, the situation was complicated by a lack of support structures. At least in the United States a handicapped individual could be institutionalized, and assured of being fed, clothed and cleaned. It Haiti, this was rare for the healthy. Consequently, what would be considered appropriate treatment in the United States was senseless in Haiti.

Epilogue

Lespwa fè viv.
Hope makes us live.

Haitian proverb

While I worked in Haiti, I learned the limitations of American medicine and technology. The problems that initially seemed so easy to solve became infinitely complex the better I understood them. There were no simple solutions. While access to contraception is important, it in itself will not decrease birth rates. Starvation can not be eradicated by importing free food. A country's economic status is a more important determinant of health care than the number of doctors or hospitals.

American health care is exceptional because the people are industrialized, prosperous, and literate, a situation that did not occur overnight. In previous generations, women died in childbirth and tuberculosis was the leading killer.

Many projects that aimed at improving health care were realistic. Most are centered in Port-au-Prince, but one can visit obscure places in Haiti and find a dedicated missionary dispensing vitamins and antibiotics. Hospitals have been established, the most famous being Albert Schweitzer Hospital in central Haiti. Serving a population of 250,000, it addresses basic health care needs. Education is given in nutrition and hygiene. Immunization and anti-tuberculosis programs have been implemented. I had the opportunity to speak with its director and he told me that he deliberately discouraged American physicians who want to perform complicated surgical procedures. It is like putting a Picasso in a house without a roof.

On the other hand, I saw organizations that imported American technology at high cost and low yield. Visiting surgeons performed corneal transplants that opacified and skin grafts that sloughed off because the patients did not receive careful postoperative care. They transported patients to the United States for sophisticated surgical treatment while ignoring the patient's long-term economic needs. While they were motivated by the best of intentions, they were not changing anything. I concluded that the best medical care that we can give is vaccinations, birth control, oral rehydration and malaria eradication.

The best people to provide health care to the Haitians are the Haitians themselves. At least fifty new physicians graduate annually from the University Hospital. Many are genuinely concerned about the plight of their people, but their idealism is blunted by a harsh economic reality: one can not make a living serving people who can not pay. They are required to spend a year of medical service helping the poor, but too often it is an exercise in futility. The clinics are located in rural areas without a phone, shower, or social life. They are poorly stocked and the available medicines are often expired. Electric power for refrigerators stops intermittently, spoiling the vaccines. No diagnostic equipment is available, and many patients just want a meal. After training, these young physicians are unable to find good-paying jobs. The market to provide care for the elite few who can pay is completely saturated.

The obvious solution is to get out of the country and that is exactly what they do. I once was invited to a party by Haitian medical students who were celebrating passing the examination that qualified them for a residency in the United States. If they obtained one, they would learn how to use CAT scans, Swan-Gantz catheters, fetal monitors and respirators. They would not become proficient at diagnosing malaria and parasitic infections let alone handling kwashiorkor and tuberculosis. Those who wanted to return and serve the poor would be inadequately trained. More important, they would realize they could have a better life in the United States – political freedom, economic opportunity and reliable utilities – and opt to stay. This "brain drain" happens not only in the medical field but in other professions too. Haiti does have a large and talented middle class but it's in New York and Miami.

There were attempts to help Haiti in other areas besides health care. Over 100 private organizations, from missionaries to independent altruists, have projects. Just about everything conceivable is being done. Schools and orphanages have been built. There are programs that teach farming, fishing, reforestation and beekeeping – a veritable gallery of development projects. I even saw one group import four water buffalos at the cost of $10,000 each to harvest rice. Each organization will rattle off statistics: how many starving children they have fed, how many farmers they have trained and how many children they have educated. But even though millions of dollars have been spent, Haiti has not improved. More are starving than ever. The poor are willing to sell all their possessions in a desperate attempt to leave the country. Haiti is a land of defunct projects. Everybody is helping, but little is being accomplished. There is no coordination, no communication; each group is in its own little act.

In spite of the odds, though, everyone, from the fundamentalist missionaries to the Peace Corps volunteers, was genuinely trying to help. But many were frustrated, too. They only saw the Haitians becoming more dependent. Those who have worked in Haiti for over a year developed a hopeless cynicism. They all had the same burnt-out look on their faces and many became alcoholics. They were "banging their heads against the wall," so to speak, because they could not change the underlying problems of injustice and inequality.

These people, like myself, had unrealistic expectations. Most Americans believe that all problems have quick solutions. When we work in a country like Haiti and discover otherwise, we are surprised – then cynical. As one Haitian merchant pointed out to me while I was obnoxiously demanding a tire for my moped. "You want everything 'vit, vit, vit'" – "fast, fast, fast." Haiti does not work like that.

Haiti does not want outside "experts" to tell it what to do. Haitians are intensely proud people and everyone from the starving peasants to the wealthy elite knew that Haiti is the only country to successfully overthrow slavery. The typical Haitian would rather starve than have a foreign government dictate their policies, especially if the people in that country's government were white. Anyone who wants to help Haiti must understand this.

Bashing Haiti for its inability to establish representative government is counterproductive. Americans tend to forget that our democratic structure required 200 years to develop in the United States and was a product of over 500 years of struggle from feudal monarchy in England. To expect a similar structure to develop in Haiti in a matter of years, even generations, is unrealistic. Unlike other

Caribbean countries that had ties with colonial powers, Haiti remained persona non grata, hindering its progress.

Nonetheless, no major improvements will come to Haiti until a political system is developed that allows people to prosper from the fruits of their labor. Although the fall of Duvalier is an important first step, the economic structure that permits the elite to parasite from the work of the peasants still exists. Perhaps a democratic structure is on the horizon, but it is unlikely to change the vast inequities that exist in Haiti quickly. Just as the babies I treated for kwashiorkor did not improve overnight, we can not expect rapid progress in Haiti. With an illiteracy rate of 80%, Haiti lacks the backbone of any healthy democracy, an educated populace.

The United States needs to patiently encourage representative government in Haiti without embarrassing its leaders by constantly subjecting them to the "white glove" test. A mini-Marshall plan needs to be instituted to coordinate the variety of projects trying to help Haiti. Most important, Haiti needs the political and economic climate to encourage the return of those who can truly build Haiti – the expatriated middle class. Haitians need to be able to travel freely between the United States and Haiti without fear of political reprisals. Haitians working in the United States should not be subject to extortion when they try to send money they have earned back to their poor families in Haiti.

It is a crime to see the Haitians in such a state. They are warm, wonderful people. Except when in dire straits, they are friendly and upbeat. They harbor little prejudice and will not physically attack foreigners. I have walked through the poorest slums of Port-au-Prince without fear. Sometimes, I even welcomed aggressiveness, like that of the taxi-driver who tried to overcharge me. Never was anything stolen from me, and once when I dropped a $10 bill while pulling out my stethoscope, an emaciated old lady wearing a black dress that most people would not use for a rag returned it to me. Haitians are truly the salt of the earth and I will always consider it my privilege to have served them.

References

Chapter 1

Program Overview: Haiti. U.S. AID, Washington D.C. October, 1982.

Haitians Sell Everything to Come to the United States. New York Times. Nov. 23, 1981, A1.

ALLDATA - Haiti. United States Agency for International Development. Washington, D.C., 1983.

Paquin, Lyonel. The Haitians: Class and Color Politics. Multi-Type. Brooklyn, NY, 1983.

Laguerre, Michel S. American Odyssey: Haitians in New York City. Cornell University Press, Ithaca, NY. 1984.

James, C.L.R. The Black Jacobins. Vintage Books, NY, 1963.

Chapter 5

Malaria Resurges in the Third World. Wall Street Journal. Jan. 15, 1981, Sec. 2, 29(W).

Chapter 6

McGuire, Robert. Bottom - Up Development in Haiti. United States Agency for International Development (organization publication). Washington D.C., 1983.

Chapter 7

Cahill, Kevin M. The AIDS Epidemic. St. Martins Press. NY, NY. 1983.

Leibowitch, Jacques. A Strange Virus of Unknown Origin. Balantine Books, NY, NY. 1984.

Pape et al. Characteristics of AIDS in Haiti. New England Journal of Medicine, vol. 309, 945-949, 1983.

Tracing the Origin of AIDS. Newsweek. May 7, 1984. 101-2.

Debate Grows of U.S. Listing of Haitians in AIDS Category. New York Times. July 31, 1983. Page 1 sec. 1.

Bazell, Robert. The History of an Epidemic. The New Republic. Aug. 1,1983, 14-18.

Cubans, Not Haitians offered Legal status. National Catholic Reporter. Feb 24, 1984. 5.

Hotels are Hit Hard as Tourists Shun Haiti. New York Times. Oct. 11, 1984. A14.

For Haiti's Tourism, the Stigma of AIDS is Fatal, New York Times. Nov. 29, 1983. A2.

Haitian Says Economy Hurt by AIDS Fear. The Washington Post. Aug 10, 1983. A9.

Haitians Removed form AIDS Risk List. New York Times. April 10, 1985. A13.

How Women May Transmit AIDS to Men is Suggested by Research. New York Times. March 7, 1986. A16.

Linking AIDS to Africa Provokes Bitter Debate. New York Times. Nov 21, 1985. A1.

Clumeck et al.(letter). Heterosexual Promiscuity Among African Patients with AIDS. New England Journal of Medicine. Vol. 313, 182.

Cinéas, F. (letter). Haitian Ambassador Deplores AIDS Connection. New England Journal of Medicine. Vol 309, 668.

The AIDS Generation. The Village Voice. May 27, 1986. 19-32.

Study Says AIDS in Haiti Spreads Mainly By Heterosexual Activity. New York Times. June 29, 1986. A1.

Chapter 8

Short, R.V. Breast Feeding. Scientific American. April, 1984. 23-29.

Urbanization. Population Reports. Johns Hopkins University. Sept-Oct, 1983.

Contraception Research Lagging. Science. Vol. 229, 1985. 1066.

A Ticking Population Bomb. Newsweek. June 25, 1984.

The Malthusian Time Bomb is Still Ticking. New York Times. July 29, 1984. E3.

Mass, Bonnie. Population Target. Charles Publishing Company, Ontario. 1976.

In Haiti, the Land is Worn Nearly to the Bone. New York Times. June 15, 1986, E3.

The Coming Crisis. New Republic. Dec, 13, 1982, 4.

Program Overview: Haiti. U.S. AID, Washington D.C. October, 1982.

Chapter 9

Population Reports: Immunizing the World's Children. Johns Hopkins Univerisity. March-April, 1986.

Measles in the Tropics. British Medical Journal. Vol 2, 1976, 1339-40.

APPENDIX

A VISIT WITH MY SON

I am sitting on a cot in the courtyard of the Children's Home run by the Missionaries of Charity in Port-au-Prince, Haiti. On my lap is a small girl who is paralyzed from polio; she moves her fingers a little but her back and legs form a dead weight. Standing beside me is Alice, whose sad little eyes and mouth appear isolated in a mass of skin eruptions and sores that cover what should be a face, as well as eroding her tiny arms and fingers. Behind me a blind baby cries for what he cannot see; I reach a free hand back to rub his spine and tiny ribs and he seems to be comforted. I begin to sing a French nursery rhyme about planting cabbages and a voice joins mine. It belongs to a girl of about seven whose pink dress covers the syphilitic sores that have resulted from the worst kind of child abuse. We sing of planting cabbages with our nose, our eyes, our ears, and most anything else I can remember in French. Five or six pairs of black eyes gaze at me from beautiful dark little faces and repeat as if in a litany, "Maman Docteur Joe, Maman Docteur Joe."

*　　*　　*　　*　　*　　*

The Docteur Joe" whose "Maman" I am is Joseph F. Bentivegna, MD, a 1978 graduate of Saint Francis College who is spending a year as a volunteer physician in the poorest country in the Americas. I have come to spend eight days with him during my spring vacation, and will describe a typical morning.

We are staying in a modest hotel where the tourist business is so bad that there are just a few guests. After a breakfast of fruit juice, a banana, bread and peanut butter and coffee, we go out to the street to hail a taxi. Joe usually travels on a motor bike wearing his brother's snowmobile helmet, but my maternal devotion, while quite deep, does not extend to mounting upon any sort of two-wheeled vehicle.

Port-au-Prince is set on a bay and surrounded by mountains. The city itself is quite hilly and resembles a cluster of villages that have somehow been joined together by winding roads to form a metropolitan area. The public transportation is most efficient, if a bit unusual. It consists of battered taxis without meters and "tap-taps." The tap-taps are pickup trucks that have been modified to seat passengers facing each other with a roof over their heads and an open rear exit. They are decorated with brightly-colored designs that include animals and birds and feature a name, almost always a religious one. They give the city the aspect of a giant child's toy box.

Any taxi ride beyond the usual route requires bargaining before one enters. Once the price is agreed upon, Joe and I join the two or three passengers that are already in the vehicle, and we all greet each other with "bon jour." As we barrel through the crowded streets, our horn blaring a warning, we somehow manage to avoid collision with man or machine as we discuss the upcoming Carnaval celebration. As a language teacher, I am impressed by Joe's fluent and lively Creole, a language he has diligently studied and practiced so as to be able to communicate with his patients. The people seem to understand my French, though I would have to spend more time in Haiti to learn to understand their language.

After a ride of about fifteen minutes, we walk up a dusty road to the Children's Home, which seems to combine a hospital with an orphanage. The nuns, wearing the characteristic sari with blue-striped trim so familiar in photos and films of Mother Teresa, are mostly from India, with two French sisters and one from Canada. A few Haitian women help the sisters care for the fifty or sixty children. The sisters follow their founder's philosophy of giving their devotion in a cheerful and loving way, speaking Creole to the children and workers and a delightful lilting English to each other and to Joe.

The young doctor first goes into the room with about nine cribs where the sickest children are located. He has treated little Chantal with a blood transfusion and nourishment through a tube into her stomach, as well as with medicine, but she still looks very sick as her mother sits by her bed to comfort her. A baby boy is so dehydrated that he cries with no tears; his legs and feet are swollen. Severe malnutrition makes it difficult for the children to fight disease, and they often cannot even produce the antibodies that cause redness in a normal reaction to infection.

A second large room is full of cribs for the infants that are getting better. They are so tiny that it is strange to see children who seem to be the size of a nine-month-old but yet are able to run around, to climb, and to feed themselves. One baby has Down's syndrome and happily flops his limbs around his crib. Little Stephan is hydrocephalic and looks like a sultan in his turban of bandages. The children spend part of the day in their cribs and part happily crawling around, socializing and playing with each other. They are very loving and affectionate.

There is still another large room with lower beds for the older children. Volunteer workers from the United States and other countries come and stay in the sisters' guest house and take turns cooking for anywhere from two weeks to several months. They help feed the infants who are too small to feed themselves and spend time rocking and playing with the children. Joe has trained some of them to set up IV's [intravenous lines] and do other medical procedures, as do the sisters themselves. An important part of his work is to diagnose illness so as to prescribe the appropriate medicines. The childish features that I remember well are still evident in the face of the physician who peers so intently into a microscope, searching for a deadly organism and planning a strategy to combat it.

Joe usually spends his afternoons at the Home for the Dying, also operated by the sisters. A description of that institution would go beyond the space allotted for this article ...

"Docteur Joe" has developed a deep affection for the Haitian people in the months that he has spent among them, a feeling that is obviously reciprocated by those whose suffering he alleviates. I was most happy to be able to share in his experiences in a small way. Both of our lives have been touched by these handsome, courteous and gentle people.

The preceding article was written by Dr. Patricia Bentivegna, Professor of Spanish at Saint Francis College (PA) and is reprinted from *The Forum* with permission. While still a college student, Dr. Bentivegna was a summer volunteer in Mexico with the American Friends Service Committee.

Index

ORDER FORM

Michelle Publishing Company
2275 Silas Deane Highway
Rocky Hill, CT 06067
Web Page - www.haitibook.com
E mail - haitibook@aol.com
860-721-8800 (Office) 860-721-1694 (Fax)

Number of Copies	Price per Copy
1	$14.95
2-5	$12.95
5-9	$11.95
10-99	$10.95
100 and over	$ 8.95

Please send me ________ copies of *The Neglected and Abused.* Please include $2.00 for postage and handling for one book and 50 cents per book for two or more not to exceed $10.00. Prices subject to change without notice. Add 25% for Canada. Do not send cash.

NAME ____

ADDRESS____

CITY ___________________________ STATE/ZIP__________

___Check Enclosed ___ Visa ___ MC

Card #____________________________ Exp. Date: _________

Signature _________________________________

Telephone _________________________________